HERITAGE UNL

Guide to free sites in Devon, D

D1335172

St Catherine's Chapel Abbotsbury, Dorset

CONTENTS

As well as its many major attractions, such as Dartmouth Castle and Cleeve Abbey, the South West is home to a wealth of English Heritage sites to which entry is free. This book, one of a series of new guidebooks, provides concise but informative introductions to each of these sites in Devon, Dorset and Somerset.

The sites are remarkably varied. Some of the most impressive prehistoric monuments in England are to be found here, including the Neolithic stone circles at Stanton Drew – the third largest collection of standing stones in England – and the massive Iron Age hillfort at Maiden Castle. There are remains from the Roman and Saxon periods, medieval gems such as the 14th-century moated castle at Nunney, and later monuments such as Dunster's Yarn Market. Settings vary from the wilderness of Dartmoor, which is littered with evidence of human habitation in prehistoric and medieval times, to busy towns and villages.

Throughout the book, special features highlight particular aspects of the area's history and character: the way in which its

Standing stone, Stanton Drew Stone Circles

landscape **WITHDRAWN** has inspired many artists and writers, for example; the extraordinary richness of Dartmoor's prehistoric remains; and the unique character of the Somerset Levels.

This guide aims to help visitors to explore, understand and enjoy some of the lesser known but intriguing monuments which are in English Heritage's care. For those who want to see more, a brief guide to English Heritage's paying sites in the area is given at the end of the book.

DEVON

No single image can capture the essence of Devon. The northern coastline is typified by dramatic headlands and surf-sprayed sands, while the south coast has sandstone cliffs, glorious beaches and sheltered bays. Inland, Dartmoor and Exmoor offer majestic views and remote wilderness, contrasting with the rolling hills, patchworks of fields, and sunken lanes of the more pastoral areas.

The national park of Dartmoor is extraordinarily rich in the relics of earlier habitation – burial chambers, standing stones, round houses, ancient field systems and tin mines. Particularly impressive are the Bronze Age settlement at Grimspound and the mysterious stone rows at Merrivale, while the remains of a deserted medieval settlement can be seen at Houndtor. Picturesque villages were once prosperous industrial centres: Lydford, on the edge of Dartmoor, originated as a Saxon fortress town, boasted a royal

mint, and was an important centre of the tin industry, its castle serving as a prison.

Fortifications on the south coast bear witness to the threat of external enemies: at the mouth of the Dart estuary the defences of Dartmouth Castle and Bayard's Cove Fort were among the earliest designed for artillery. Further south, Plymouth has been the base of the navy since the time of the Spanish Armada.

Opposite: Houndtor Deserted Medieval Village

Map labels:
- Unstaffed sites
- Staffed sites
- Lydford Castle & Saxon Town
- Okehampton Castle
- Blackbury Camp
- Grimspound
- Houndtor
- Merrivale
- Upper Plym Valley
- Totnes Castle
- Berry Pomeroy Castle
- Kirkham House
- Royal Citadel
- Bayard's Cove Fort
- Dartmouth Castle

Right: Bayard's Cove Fort

Opposite: Detail from a map of about 1539, showing the fortifications guarding the Dart estuary. Dartmouth Castle is the large castle on the west bank near the river mouth, and Bayard's Cove Fort can be clearly seen just north-west of the castle

History

Bayard's Cove Fort was built in the early 16th century by the townspeople of Dartmouth to protect the town quay. The significance of its strategic position is best appreciated from the sea: it controls the narrowest point of the channel at the entrance to Dartmouth harbour.

The town of Dartmouth developed in the Middle Ages because of the value of the safe, deep water anchorage at the mouth of the Dart estuary. It was here in the estuary that the English contingent assembled in 1147 and again in 1190 to depart on crusade. Originally, the major port on the River Dart was Totnes, higher upriver, but from the 13th century the name Dartmouth was being used for the harbour town that was gradually expanding south along the waterside. The town became the main base for the wine trade with south-west France, and despite the loss of this source of wealth following the start of the Hundred Years' War (1337–1453), Dartmouth continued to prosper with the growth of the cloth trade.

The fort may have been built as early as 1509–10 according to contemporary documents, and was certainly in existence by 1537, when it is mentioned as the 'New Castle' in a corporation lease. On the southern edge of the town, it stands at the end of a stone quay which was also constructed early in the 16th century. Nearer the harbour mouth, Dartmouth Castle and its companion fort across the estuary, Kingswear Castle, had already been built in the late 15th century to guard the port. Fearful of

7

attack, the people of Dartmouth decided to built Bayard's Cove Fort as a second line of defence, in case an enemy succeeded in evading the guns of Dartmouth and Kingswear.

When Dartmouth eventually came under attack – during the English Civil War, more than a century after the fort had been built – the enemy came not, as expected, from the sea, but from the land. Dartmouth declared for Parliament but was captured in 1643 by a Royalist force under Prince Maurice after a month's siege. The Royalists built new gun forts on the hilltops overlooking Dartmouth and Kingswear, but in 1646 they surrendered to the Parliamentarian New Model Army after a brisk assault under cover of darkness. A Parliamentarian recorded that 'we became masters of the whole Town, and the old Castle [Bayard's Cove] in which were 5 great Iron guns which commanded the River'.

During the 18th century, Dartmouth went through a period of decline and the area around the fort became an overcrowded slum. Recovery began with the arrival of the Royal Naval College in 1863, and the growth of tourism. Bayard's Cove Fort was rescued from the state of neglect into which it had fallen and for a brief interval in 1940 was adapted as a machine gun post. It was quickly abandoned for the same weakness that marked its construction: the restricted field of fire from the gunports. Since 1984 it has been in the care of English Heritage.

The Dart estuary, seen from above Bayard's Cove

Bayard's Cove Fort was never tested in a naval assault, but it rapidly became obsolete as the type of cannon for which it was designed was replaced by new and more powerful weaponry. Though the potential of artillery was recognised at an early stage, at the outset it was unreliable and often ineffective. Casting was one problem overcome in Henry VIII's reign with improved iron manufacture; the rate at which cannon could be reloaded and fired also improved. The result was a new kind of castle like those at St Mawes and Pendennis in Cornwall (built 1540–45). Low and massive, they represent the climax of a process of development in which forts like Bayard's Cove were an important intermediate stage.

Description

The fort is irregular in plan but simple in design. It consists of a high, thick wall enclosing a roughly rectangular space with rounded corners, some 10m (33 ft) across. The original entrance was on the north side and survives as a much damaged pointed archway with a drip moulding above. Access to a narrow wall-walk was via a stone stairway climbing over the entrance arch. The fort wall was originally topped by a parapet, mostly now missing, from which musketeers or archers could fire. The wall-walk gave access to a small area just west of the rock face where the gunners' accommodation might have been sited: traces of lean-to buildings can be seen in the rock face here.

Below, a row of eleven gunports close to the water's edge allowed heavy guns to be brought to bear on enemy ships. At this time, cannon were generally fixed to heavy wooden base-plates, rather than mounted on wheels. The gunports are larger than those at Dartmouth Castle, which was the first English castle purpose-built with gunports to take heavy guns: they are similar in design, with internal splays and external slots for shutters.

A working replica from Dartmouth Castle of the type of gun for which Bayard's Cove Fort was designed

In Dartmouth on the river front (signposted)
OS Map 202;
ref SX 879509

9

A BRONZE AGE LANDSCAPE:

Many visitors to Dartmoor are unaware of the wonderfully well preserved archaeological remains that survive in abundance throughout the area. Taken together, they represent one of the nation's greatest archaeological landscapes, and provide a crucial insight into the character, lives and rituals of peoples who once lived there.

The best known archaeological remains on Dartmoor are those dating from prehistoric times. Foremost among these are the widespread and extremely well preserved remains of entire Bronze Age landscapes, complete with settlements, field systems, ritual areas and burial grounds. Archaeologists are continuing to find significant numbers of previously unknown sites, and as a result our picture of life during the Bronze Age (*c*2300–700 BC) on Dartmoor is still developing.

Currently the remains of over 900 settlements are known, varying in size from a few houses to sites comprising over one hundred surviving buildings. Associated with most of these settlements are field systems in which crops were grown and animals grazed, although many are built within enclosures used to control livestock. An excellent example of an enclosed settlement survives at Grimspound (page 14) and several others can be found within the Upper Plym Valley (page 28).

Above: *The Bronze Age settlement at Grimspound*
Right: *The prehistoric enclosures and round houses on the western slopes of Trowlesworthy Tor in the Upper Plym Valley, seen from the air*

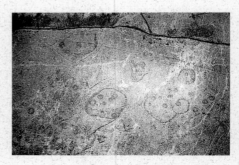

Settlements with field systems tend to contain fewer houses, but they are generally much more substantial. The field systems themselves vary considerably in character, but among the most impressive are the coaxial examples, where groups of fields are arranged on one main axis, subdivided by transverse boundaries and defined by a terminal reave or bank at either end. The two largest examples each extend over 3,000 hectares and show that the impact of Bronze Age farmers on the Dartmoor landscape was considerable.

Ritual played an important part in the lives and deaths of the people who worked on Dartmoor in the Bronze Age. The remains of at least 18 stone circles and 70 stone rows testify to ceremonial activities. The precise nature of the ceremonies practised cannot now be established, but over the years various ideas have evolved to explain the character and distribution of these often impressive monuments. At Merrivale (page 26) a group of stone rows and a stone circle testify to the importance of this as a ritual area during prehistoric times.

The purpose of the thousands of burial cairns or mounds is clearer, although again their place in the ritual and territorial world of the Bronze Age has been the subject of debate. Within many of the cairns, small stone coffins known as cists were built to contain the dead, and within the Shavercombe area of the Upper Plym Valley numerous fine cists have been revealed by antiquarians and treasure hunters.

Towards the end of the Bronze Age a mixture of climatic and soil deterioration led to many of the settlements, their fields and ritual areas being abandoned. We can only wonder at the turmoil and hardship endured by the people who have left us such a remarkable legacy.

Part of one of the double stone rows at Merrivale

BLACKBURY CAMP

Blackbury Camp, or Castle, is one of many similar sites across southern Britain dating from the period known as the Iron Age (*c*800 BC to the 1st century AD). A favourite place for picnics, it is now hidden within woodland, which makes its appearance in the Iron Age hard to imagine.

The rampart surrounding Blackbury Camp

The lowland areas of Devon and Cornwall are densely scattered with Iron Age settlements. They offered richer soils than the moorland sites favoured in earlier times. Most of these Iron Age hillforts or settlements are located on hill slopes or at the end of ridges, overlooking springs or river valleys, probably for pastoral rather than defensive purposes. Blackbury Camp is no exception: it straddles a narrow ridge running eastwards from a plateau, near the junction of two ancient tracks. This position gave good access to valley pastures and to two nearby streams, although it was not easily fortified.

The enclosure at Blackbury is oval in shape, roughly 200m (660 ft) long by 100m (330 ft) wide. Surrounding it is an impressive rampart, now about 3m (10 ft) high and up to 10m (33 ft) wide. This is built from clay and flints quarried from an outer ditch which measures up to 12m (39 ft) wide.

The single entrance on the south side is defined by large ramparts. It was about 5m (16 ft) wide and would originally have been revetted with timber and contained a large gateway with timber gates, possibly set within a timber gate-tower. The ground surface around the entrance was gravelled with pebbles from the stream below, suggesting that heavy use was expected during the wetter months of the year. Three other gaps in the rampart are thought to be more recent features.

The most remarkable feature of Blackbury Camp is the earthwork in front of the entrance, which is triangular in shape, and flanked by a bank and ditch. Settlements of this period usually have additional, outer enclosures, but these are normally arranged in concentric circles around the main one. We do not know whether the outer enclosure at Blackbury was intended to be defensive or whether it had a practical use, perhaps as a holding area for cattle.

The site was excavated in the 1950s, when the finds included the remains of a hut, various trenches, a cooking pit, an oven, pottery and a

hoard of over 1,000 slingstones. Parts of two rectangular structures built against the inner face of the rampart may be the remains of medieval or later buildings. The Iron Age pottery that was found is simple and made from the local Greensand clays. It is most likely that settlements like Blackbury were the defended homesteads of the wealthier members of society: the inner enclosure would have been the area where the owner and family lived, while the outer enclosure was probably designed to protect the homestead pastures and watering places.

One of the gaps in the rampart of the hillfort

5 miles NW of Seaton. Signposted from A3052 Sidmouth–Lyme Regis, about halfway between Sidford and Colyford
OS Map 192; ref SY 187924

13

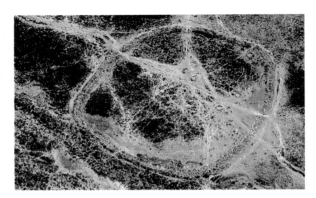

Above: An aerial view of Grimspound from the north. The original entrance is at the top

Below: The entrance to the enclosure

History

Grimspound is one of the best known prehistoric settlements on Dartmoor, probably dating from the Late Bronze Age (*c*1450–700 BC). The remains of 24 houses enclosed within a stone wall, and further houses outside the enclosure, lie in a fold in the hills about 450m (1,500 ft) above sea level, between Hookney and Hameldown tors.

The earlier Neolithic period, from about 4500 BC, witnessed a transition from a hunting and gathering lifestyle towards a growing reliance on farming. By 2500 BC the early farmers were moving into upland areas like Dartmoor, and settled farms and field systems were becoming commonplace. The remains of the characteristic round houses (also known as hut circles) in which people lived can still be seen – sometimes standing on their own, like isolated cottages today; sometimes, as here, grouped together in sizeable villages. Such settlements are a defining feature of the Dartmoor landscape.

We do not know precisely how long Grimspound was in use, but by about 1200 BC the settlement pattern was changing. The thin moorland soils appear to have deteriorated very quickly and it also seems that there was a change in the climate. Heavy rainfall reduced the fertility of the Dartmoor soil, so that it could not sustain the same level of occupation.

Grimspound was excavated at the end of the 19th century by the newly formed Dartmoor Exploration Committee. They excavated 16 of the houses and found numerous structures and artefacts, including porches, paved floors, hearths, raised benches, cooking holes, charcoal, pottery and flint. However, no organic matter which might date the site was recovered. The excavators restored parts of the perimeter wall and some of the hut circles, although not very accurately.

A reconstruction painting of Grimspound from the south-west, by Ivan Lapper

Description

The great boundary wall is about 150m (500 ft) in diameter. Averaging 3m (10 ft) thick and standing up to 1.5m (5 ft) high, it is faced with large slabs laid in horizontal courses, with a core of smaller stones between the two faces. However, it seems unlikely that it was intended to be defensive – it was probably simply a barrier to keep wild animals out and farmed animals in. The site overlooks a valley to the north where there was open grazing land, but the original entrance was on the opposite, uphill side. This imposing entrance is flanked by high walls, with a passage 1.8m (6 ft) wide which is roughly paved. A stream running through the northern half of the enclosure would have provided an excellent supply of fresh water, and explains the settlement's position.

The walls of the houses within the enclosure were probably not much higher than they are now, and covered with conical roofs of turf or thatch. A number of low rubble banks against the internal face of the enclosure wall probably formed sheep or cattle pens. Immediately south-east of the enclosure the remains of at least nine more houses survive, all linked to rubble banks forming part of a field system.

You can climb up Hookney Tor for a good view of the site, and the high ground on Hameldown is another good vantage point.

6 miles SW of Moretonhampstead, S along minor road off B3212 at Shapley Common: the site is on the left after 1½ miles
OS Map 191; ref SX 701809

History

The fine remains of this abandoned and isolated settlement lie on the eastern edge of Dartmoor, between the granite landmarks of Hound Tor and Greator Rocks. The village, which was excavated in the 1960s, consists of a cluster of rectangular longhouses and barns which were shown to date from the 13th century, though the area may have been used for summer grazing during the Roman period. There is evidence that the area was farmed during the Bronze Age, and it may have been first farmed even earlier.

During the Middle Ages a combination of population growth and favourable weather seems to have encouraged people to move higher up on to the moor, taking in marginal land that was normally too difficult to cultivate. Animals were an important element in this kind of husbandry – oxen to pull the ploughs, cattle for meat and milk, and sheep for meat and woollen clothing. Medieval farmers liked to bring their beasts indoors, creating the typical Dartmoor longhouse – a rectangular building in which the family lived at one end and the animals at the other. There were at least four of these in the hamlet at Houndtor.

The life of the permanent settlement may have been short. Pollen evidence suggests that cereal farming had ceased by 1350, but a recent re-examination of the pottery suggests occupation to the end of the 14th or early 15th century.

Houndtor from the north

Description

Today the first set of foundations you reach from the car park to the north-west are those of a barn, with a corn drying oven and a kiln. A little further on lies the first of the four longhouses, which had a small lean-to to the left of the door. A passage dividing people from animals is clearly marked by the two entrances, and a drainage channel identifies the area for livestock. To the right, an additional room opens out from the back of the main family accommodation.

Continuing eastwards, the second and third longhouses are similar in plan. One of the doorways in the third house has been blocked, and the exterior suggests that this was done when the building was converted into a farm building. Beyond lies the largest building on the site, sometimes inaccurately called a manor house. It had a garden and two smaller associated buildings, perhaps the homes of dependants or labourers. Two further rectangular buildings at the southern edge of the village may also have been

The remains of the largest house, looking towards Hound Tor

dwellings. Behind them is an open area with faint traces of ploughing, probably 19th-century rather than medieval.

The walls of the houses were made of granite boulders from the surrounding moor, possibly rendered in some way on the inside. None stands high enough now to show the positions of windows. Roofs would have been thatched with rushes or straw, and smoke from the open central hearth dispersed through the eaves.

From the top of Greator Rocks, there is an excellent view back over the village and the medieval strip field system around it.

1¹/₂ miles S of Manaton, on minor road signposted Houndtor/ Swallerton Gate off B3344; ¹/₂ mile walk from Hound Tor car park OS Map 191; ref SX 746788

KIRKHAM HOUSE

History

Kirkham House is a well-preserved late medieval house, built of local stone. It lies near the centre of the town of Paignton, which 500 years ago was a small village clustered around its parish church, not far from the palace of the bishops of Exeter. Today Kirkham House stands in a crowded back street opposite new housing of starkly contrasting character. From outside it is hard to imagine it as it once was, probably rendered and limewashed, and surrounded by buildings of a similar nature. Step inside the house, however, and it is possible to forget some of the 21st-century bustle.

Although it was once known as the Priest's House, it is more likely to have been the house of a well-to-do landowning or merchant family: the detailing inside the house suggests that it belonged to someone of high status. There are no documents to tell us exactly when or by whom it was built. The carving on the woodwork suggests a 14th-century date, but the layout of the house is more typical of the 15th century, when a growing desire for privacy led to the creation of separate rooms for different domestic activities. It has the traditional three-room plan found in rural farmhouses of this date.

Description

Entrance to the house is through a fine arched oak doorway, added in the 16th century to bring the house more up to date. Beyond lies a typical

The parlour

medieval screens passage, giving access to the hall on the right and a parlour on the left. Each room has a fine hooded fireplace. The parlour is elaborately finished and was probably intended for business use, though it may also have been used for private relaxation. There was once an ornate stone washbasin here, but it has been removed and taken to the parish church in Goodrington.

The hall was intended for more formal occasions, with enough space for the whole household – perhaps as many as 20 people – to dine together. Food came via the screens passage from an outside kitchen (now ruined). As in the parlour there was originally a finely carved washbasin here, which is now in the vestry of Paignton parish church.

Beyond the hall lies a separate unheated room which once had its own outside doorway. This may have been a store, or even a shop, at some period in its history.

A staircase from the parlour leads to the three upper rooms. Above the

The second chamber on the first floor, furnished with a modern bed

parlour is the best chamber, and this gives access to a small second chamber, which is partly jettied out over the hall below. A gallery, added in the 16th century, leads to a third chamber at the far end of the house, with its own garderobe and an attic above. These two rooms originally had their own outside staircase and may have been intended for use by servants.

Today a number of examples of modern furniture are displayed in the house, to illustrate traditional English timber and joinery techniques.

In Kirkham St, off Cecil Rd, Paignton. Please phone for opening times: 0870 333 1181 Open in association with the Paignton Preservation and Local History Society
OS Map 202; ref SX 885610

19

GREAT ESTATES:

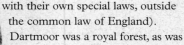

The arrival of the Normans in England in 1066 led to the development of a system of land ownership dependent on control by the Crown and the aristocracy. An estate provided the owner not only with income from land or rent from tenants, but also with a residence – usually a castle – and a setting commensurate with the owner's social standing and wealth. Ownership of land has long brought with it political power. When Henry III (reigned 1216–72) gave vast tracts of land in Devon and Cornwall to his brother Richard, Earl of Cornwall, it was part of a princely endowment to support Richard's attempt to become Holy Roman Emperor.

Royal estates in Norman times included vast tracts of forest (not necessarily wooded, for the term 'forest' applied to lands set apart with their own special laws, outside the common law of England). Dartmoor was a royal forest, as was the forest of Gillingham in Dorset.

Great lords or ecclesiastics acquired rights from the Crown that gave them the right to hunt in areas known as chases: Cranborne Chase, for example, was granted to the Earl of Gloucester by William Rufus (reigned 1087–1100). These were coveted as evidence of status, but were also valuable as a source of food.

Perhaps the greatest landowner of medieval times was the church. Glastonbury Abbey was one of the richest of all English monasteries and owned land scattered throughout England, especially in Somerset, Dorset and Wiltshire. The commissioners at the Dissolution reported that 'the house is great and goodly, and so princely as we have not seen the like; with 4 parks adjoining … [and] 4 fair manor places'. The vast barns built by the monasteries clearly demonstrate the extent of monastic estates.

Above: The seal of Richard, Earl of Cornwall, one of the largest landowners in Devon and Cornwall in the 13th century
Left: The vast monastic barn at Abbotsbury, left intact after the Dissolution

After the Dissolution of the Monasteries in the 1530s, even if the other monastic buildings were destroyed, the barns, like that at Abbotsbury in Dorset, were left standing because of their importance to farming.

When the monasteries were closed at the Dissolution the Crown had a new source of land and property to bestow on those individuals it favoured. Some of the lucky recipients took possession of complete monastic estates, and converted their buildings to secular use, as at Buckland Abbey in Devon; others used the opportunity to build new residences.

The 18th century witnessed a fashion for landscape gardening on the grandest scale. At Milton Abbas in Dorset, so keen was Lord Milton (later Earl of Dorchester) to create the perfect pastoral setting for his mansion that he removed a small town in order to lay out an elegant park and lake to designs by Capability Brown. Servants and the townspeople were relocated to the model village of Milton Abbas, designed by William Chambers, a good half mile away and out of sight of the mansion.

Creation of new country estates and houses continued up until the 'golden age' of country house building before the First World War. But thereafter the combined effects of agricultural depression, taxes, death duties, loss of male heirs in the war and all the subsequent economic and social changes brought about the breakup of numerous large estates. Many estates and their houses were given over to the care of the state or the National Trust. However, some owners managed to hold on, and today they, together with English Heritage, the National Trust, and other bodies have either developed their country houses and estates as visitor attractions or found other ways of generating income, so securing them for the future.

The village of Milton Abbas, rebuilt by William Chambers in the 18th century

History

The village of Lydford has an unforgettable setting on the western edge of Dartmoor National Park, just upriver from the spectacular Lydford Gorge. Its importance in Saxon and medieval times has left its legacy in the street layout and in two castles: a post-Conquest castle, of which the earthworks remain, and a 13th-century tower, built on top of a 12th-century predecessor. This latter castle served as a prison for enforcing the laws that regulated both Dartmoor's forest and also its important tin industry.

In the 9th century Lydford, or *Llidan*, is documented as one of four important towns or burhs in Devon, its streets laid out in a grid pattern still evident in the village today, where modern hedges and footpaths fossilise the courses of earlier streets. By the 10th century the town had its own mint, and its prosperity – probably founded on profits from the tin trade – is evident from the fact that it paid as much in taxes to the king as Totnes or Barnstaple. It occupied a position of great natural strength, a triangular promontory protected on two sides by deep river valleys. The third side was defended by an earthen rampart, the remains of which can be seen as you enter the village from the north-east on either side of the road, near the

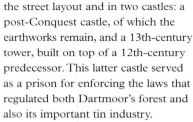

Lydford from the north-east. The 13th-century castle is just right of centre, with the earthwork castle beyond it, and the Saxon earthwork defences in the foreground

village hall. These strong defences may have been the reason that an attack by the Vikings in AD 997 was repelled.

Soon after the siege and capture of Exeter by William the Conqueror in 1068, a small defensive earthwork was built on the extreme south-west tip of the promontory at Lydford. Excavations have revealed the remains of five wooden buildings protected behind a crescent-shaped earth and timber rampart with a deep ditch. This rare early Norman castle, now owned by the National Trust, is a fascinating site and well worth visiting.

The early castle was probably abandoned fairly quickly. Meanwhile, Lydford had become the administrative centre of the forest of Dartmoor, a royal jurisdiction with important and lucrative rights. In 1194 King John authorised the building of a new tower east of the church, to house offenders against both the forest and stannary laws. Such was the importance of the tin industry in Devon and Cornwall that a special legal and taxation system had evolved to govern it, and the stannaries, or tin districts of Devon, were administered from Lydford. In 1239 Henry III granted Lydford to his brother Richard, Earl of Cornwall, as part of a princely endowment.

On the death of Earl Richard's son, Edmund, in 1300 the estate reverted to the Crown and since 1337 Dartmoor and Lydford Castle have formed part of the possessions of the Duchy of Cornwall. Offenders against the stannary laws continued to be incarcerated at the castle throughout the Middle Ages and fitfully until the 18th century. The best-known was Richard Strode, MP for Plymouth, himself a tinner, who was thrown in the gaol in 1510 after having the temerity to complain that mining debris in the moorland rivers was silting up the harbour at Plymouth. He later described his accommodation here as 'one of the most annoious, contagious and detestable places wythin this realme'.

By 1650 Lydford Castle was described as 'very much in decay', with floors fallen in and only the roof

A Saxon penny excavated at Lydford, bearing the head of King Ethelred II the Unready (reigned 978–1016)

The tower of Lydford Castle

intact. Repairs were carried out in 1716 and 1733, but by the early 19th century the place was a near ruin. But the stannary court's evil reputation for rough justice, though possibly unfounded, was long remembered. Even in the heat of summer, the bare walls and gloomy interior of Lydford Castle seem to bear witness to the words of the Devon poet William Browne (1590–1645):

> *I oft have heard of Lydford Law*
> *How in the morn they hang and draw*
> *And sit in judgement after.*

Description

King John's castle or gaol seems to have consisted of a single tower two storeys high and about 15m (50 ft) square. Its walls were more than 3m (10 ft) thick and it had deeply splayed, round-headed windows.

During the late 13th century, when the castle was gaining importance as a stannary gaol, the tower was drastically rebuilt. The upper storey was demolished and the ground floor used as the foundation for a much taller building. Earth was piled around its walls, so that the tower appears to have been built on a motte or mound. A large earthwork enclosure or bailey was formed to the north-west of the tower. Apart from a small pit in one corner, all the interior of the original ground floor was filled in, so blocking the original windows. The break between the 12th- and 13th-century work is easy to see, as the walls of the basement are much thicker than those above. Rows of joist holes indicate floor levels, and corbels near the top of the walls show where the roof timbers rested.

Entry to the tower was by a large doorway facing the bailey, from which a narrow flight of steps within the thickness of the wall led up to a large hall. In the entrance to the hall is a hole for a drawbar to secure the door; by the side of the same opening is a latrine with the ledge for its seat still in position. There may also have been apartments for the keeper or gaoler on this upper floor, with prison cells below – the pit in the basement probably being reserved for the most loathsome of prisoners.

The church of St Petroc, next to the castle, is an early Christian foundation dedicated to one of the most popular Celtic saints of the South West.

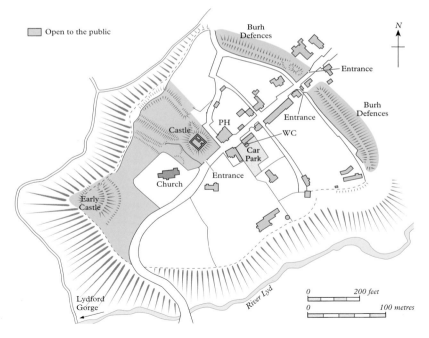

Plan of the town, banks and castles

In Lydford, off A386, 8 miles S of Okehampton OS Map 201; Saxon banks: ref SX 511849; castle: ref SX 509848

The southern double row looking west

The Dartmoor landscape is rich in prehistoric antiquities, preserved by the abandonment of the high moor when poor weather and the build-up of peat in the soil made further cultivation impossible. The group of monuments at Merrivale, where a settlement site and ritual complex lie side by side, is one of the finest on the moor. It is also one of the most accessible, being close to a road.

Merrivale includes many of the archaeological features associated with the Neolithic to Middle Bronze Age (*c*2500–1000 BC). The monuments here comprise a group of round houses; two double stone rows and one single row; a small stone circle, with two standing stones nearby; and a number of cairns (earthen mounds), associated with burials.

Nearest to the road is the area of a typical Bronze Age settlement, a large cluster of round houses. The huge rounded stone here, often mistaken for a chambered tomb, is in fact a post-medieval apple-crusher stone, used in the process of cider-making. South of the settlement and running east–west are two double stone rows, separated by a stream: each consists of more than 150 stones, mostly under a metre high. The northern double row is 182m (596 ft) long, with an average width between the rows of 1m (3 ft). The second row runs roughly parallel with the first but is longer, stretching 263m (865 ft) across the moor. It has terminal stones blocking each end. Near the middle of this row a ring of stones marks the kerb of a small cairn: this unusual feature may mark the burial of an important person.

A few metres south is a stone-lined burial chamber or cist with a massive, though damaged, capstone. Further west and just to the south of the row, a cairn marks the start of a single row of stones, running for about 40m (132 ft) at an angle to the double row.

To the west of these rows is a circle of 11 low-lying stones of local granite, about 18m (60 ft) in diameter. There is a tall stone, or menhir, nearby, which at more than 3m (10 ft) high is the most conspicuous object in the area.

It is quite possible that the ritual monuments of the Merrivale landscape belong to several different periods. In what way they might be related is a matter of conjecture, but such a vast array of monuments indicates that the site was of great spiritual importance to the people who lived in the area. Whatever ceremonies were held here, the amount of planning, motivation and organisation that went into creating such a complex of sites is astonishing. Stone rows have been described as the most distinctive monuments of prehistoric Dartmoor: there are at least 70 examples, often built in conjunction with cairns as at Merrivale.

Running west of the site is the Great Western Reave, the longest of the many reaves – earth or stone banks, probably representing ancient field boundaries – that are a distinctive feature of Dartmoor, many of them stretching for miles across the moor.

Above: The apple-crusher stone

Below left: Some of the houses of the Bronze Age settlement, seen from the air

I mile E of Merrivale off B3357 Tavistock–Princetown road, 5 miles E of Tavistock
OS Map 191; ref SX 554748

The Dartmoor landscape contains the greatest concentration of prehistoric and later archaeological sites in western Europe. This remarkable survival is due largely to the fact that the local granite, which was used for most of the structures, is so durable. A further factor has been the lack of agricultural or industrial activity on the moor in modern times, which has meant that many of the prehistoric and later monuments have been left undisturbed. One particular area, the

The remains of a Bronze Age settlement near Trowlesworthy Tor

Upper Plym Valley, has an extraordinary concentration of stone remains littered over 15.5 square km (6 square miles), making it one of the richest archaeological landscapes of Dartmoor. The area lies on the south bank of the river and extends from the source of the Plym as far as the china clay pits at Lee Moor, a distance of some 7km (4.5 miles).

Most of the remains belong to two major periods of activity on the moor: the Bronze Age (*c*2300–700 BC) and the Middle Ages. Some indication of the level of activity that once took place here was provided by an archaeological field survey undertaken between 2001 and 2002, when more than 300 monuments dating chiefly from these two periods were recorded.

The Bronze Age

There are especially well-preserved concentrations of Bronze Age settlements and enclosures on Trowlesworthy, Willings Walls and Hentor warrens. The enclosures can be seen as low, fragmentary walls of

large boulders and the settlements as hut circles, with small terraces in the hillsides enclosed by low rubble or slab walls. There are also many funerary monuments, represented by small, roughly circular cairns or mounds. The best-preserved examples contain box-like burial chambers made of granite slabs, and have retaining circles of upright slabs around them. A pair of stone rows lies on the gentle slope 0.5km south of Great Trowlesworthy Tor. One, consisting of two parallel lines of upright stones, has a small stone circle of eight stones at its northern end. Dartmoor has a greater concentration of surviving stone rows than anywhere else in Britain, but their purpose largely remains an enigma. Along with stone circles and some of the more elaborate funerary monuments they form what must have been deeply significant ritual areas, possibly the scenes of religious ceremonies.

Some of the most distinctive Bronze Age remains on Dartmoor are the low, stony, earth-covered banks known as reaves. Made up of granite boulders and layers of turf, these were probably property boundaries, and can be seen running for miles across the moorland. Over 200km (125 miles) of reaves have been identified on the moor. A good example here is Trowlesworthy reave, which crosses the moor on the hillside below Shell Top. Elsewhere on the moor and on its fringes, many field boundaries in use today still follow ancient reaves.

The double stone row at Trowlesworthy

Medieval and Later Remains

There is a notable absence in the Upper Plym Valley, as elsewhere on Dartmoor, of remains from the Iron Age and Roman periods. Archaeologists have speculated that this might relate to a deterioration in the weather, leading to a retreat to the lower and more easily farmed areas. However, whether because of more favourable weather conditions or population expansion, there is much evidence of occupation and activity in medieval times. The lower, western, end of the Upper Plym Valley was gradually resettled from the 13th century, and at least six farms or smallholdings were established in the area up to the 18th century. Of these only the earliest, Trowlesworthy, established in 1272, remains in use. The farmhouses are all of a similar design, a long rectangular building with a single entrance in the southern side. Around them are often smaller ancillary buildings and beyond these are the remains of their fields. At Hentor the fields contain the most complete examples of ridge and furrow (strip cultivation) on Dartmoor.

From the 16th century most of the farms in the Upper Plym Valley were converted into rabbit warrens. The rabbits, much valued for their meat and fur, were housed in low, rectangular earthen mounds known as pillow mounds: several hundred of these are scattered all over the Trowlesworthy and Hentor areas. The small, cross-shaped lines of stone built up against walls and enclosures within the warrens

The medieval field system at Hentor

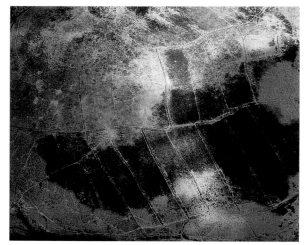

are the remains of traps used to catch vermin which might attack the rabbits: the walls encouraged foraging animals into the long stone traps, which had slate shutters operated by the animals tripping a mechanism of levers and string.

All along the floodplain of the Plym are ridges of stone and massive delvings into the river deposits. These are evidence of the tin-streaming industry that once flourished here and in the valleys all over Dartmoor, certainly from the 12th century and possible even in prehistory. The granite of the moor, as elsewhere in the South West, contains casserite (tin dioxide ore) which could be washed out of the gravel of the stream beds. As the valley was worked, large amounts of waste gravel accumulated, and were piled into stone banks. The tin ore was taken away to be crushed at stamping mills – one

of which lies just above the confluence of the Plym and Shavercombe Brook – and smelted at workshops known as blowing houses. The remains of one blowing house are visible higher up the valley where the Langcombe Brook joins the Plym.

Today the Upper Plym Valley is a typically treeless Dartmoor landscape, grazed by cattle, sheep and ponies. It is hard to imagine it 3,500 years ago dotted with settlements of neat round huts, with fields of crops growing near the river and herds of pasturing animals on the higher slopes; or, in medieval and later times, alive with the activity of rabbit farming and tin streaming.

A pillow mound, from the 14th-century Luttrell Psalter

Below left: *A 16th-century woodcut showing tin streaming*

Park at Cadover Bridge, 4 miles E of Yelverton, and walk up the track to the left of the bridge for about 1½ miles (take care: the ground may be boggy) OS Map 202; ref SX 580660

DORSET

Bordering the south coast of England, Dorset is a county of outstanding natural beauty and of strong contrasts. Its dramatic coastline, rich in fossil finds, has recently been awarded World Heritage status. The countryside inland is characterised by rolling hills, winding lanes and sleepy villages. There is a strong sense here of being in an ancient and long inhabited landscape.

The nature of the Dorset countryside is known to many through the work of Thomas Hardy, who immortalised it in his novels. The traditional rural scene he described, dependent on a pastoral economy, had survived almost unchanged for hundreds of years. As a result, the landscape is rich in ancient remains – from Neolithic stone circles such as Kingston Russell and the Nine Stones, to Bronze Age barrows and Iron Age hillforts. Maiden Castle near Dorchester is the largest Iron Age hillfort in Europe.

Lasting reminders of the impact of the Norman Conquest survive throughout Dorset. A motte-and-bailey castle and keep survive at Christchurch Castle. More modest examples of medieval architecture can been seen at Knowlton – where a medieval church sits within a Neolithic earthwork – and the wonderfully sited St Catherine's Chapel at Abbotsbury.

Left: Fishermen on Chesil Beach
Opposite: Part of the western entrance, Maiden Castle

Right: The surviving gable end of one of the monastic buildings

Below: An early 13th-century effigy of an abbot, from the parish church of St Nicholas, Abbotsbury

History

The abbey of St Peter at Abbotsbury housed a Benedictine community founded in 1044 by Orc, a house steward of King Cnut. Its layout probably followed the normal Benedictine pattern of that time, with the monastic buildings grouped around a cloister to the south of the church. Within the walled precinct of the abbey, up to 30 black-robed monks followed the orderly routine of work, study and prayer laid down for them in St Benedict's rule, saying mass for the soul of their founder and for the souls of anyone else generous enough to donate property to the community.

Very little is known of the early monastery, as much of it was demolished in Norman times: the remains now visible date from the 13th and 14th centuries. The abbey was dissolved in 1539 and the buildings were leased to Sir Giles Strangeways, who may have turned part of them into a residence. One small part is now in the care of English Heritage. The famous swannery nearby, now an

internationally famous nature reserve, was once an important source of income for the abbey, and a reminder of the wealth of the medieval monastic orders. Despite their vows of poverty, some monks lived very well, as typified by Chaucer's monk in the *Canterbury Tales*:

> *He was not pale as a tormented ghost*
> *A fat swan loved he best of any roast.*

Description

At first sight, little remains of the great abbey that gave Abbotsbury its name. However, a closer look reveals a number of buildings that together are a reminder that this was once an important and wealthy monastery.

Fragments of the abbey church can be traced in the churchyard to the south of the present parish church, but nothing survives of the cloisters, dormitory or refectory (the monks' dining room). All that remains is one gable, or end wall, of a narrow building which might have formed part of the abbot's lodging. On its inner face are two fireplaces. A short distance away are two outbuildings (not open to the public) with medieval windows: the more easterly of these buildings might have been the end of a range of lodgings for guests, entertained in accordance with the Benedictine tradition of hospitality.

The abbey's great tithe barn, dating from the 14th century, lies at the end of a path from the car park beside the abbey's fish ponds. Nearly 80m (262 ft) long, this barn (see page 20) was once one of the largest in England, with two porches, each with a watching chamber over the entrance. The capacity of the tithe barn is a convincing witness to the abbey's wealth. Today, only half of the barn is still roofed.

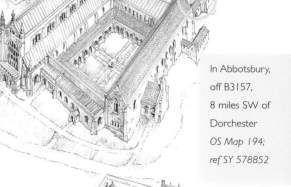

An aerial reconstruction of Abbotsbury Abbey in the late Middle Ages, by Philip Corke. The position of the gable end opposite is circled

In Abbotsbury, off B3157, 8 miles SW of Dorchester
OS Map 194; ref SY 578852

History

St Catherine's Chapel was built by the monks of nearby Abbotsbury Abbey as a pilgrimage chapel. Virtually unaltered since, it is one of a handful of chapels of this kind which are located outside the precincts of the monasteries that built them. Its isolated setting allowed the monks to withdraw from the monastery during Lent for private prayer and meditation.

St Catherine's Chapel, looking across Chesil Beach towards Portland Bill

The dedication of the chapel to St Catherine of Alexandria is rare, but her cult was one of the most popular in medieval England. The fireworks known as catherine wheels commemorate her torture in the 3rd century AD, when the Roman Emperor Maximus I ordered her to be broken on a wheel set with sword points for protesting about the persecution of Christians. An angel is said to have broken the wheel, and after her subsequent execution Catherine's body was said to have been conveyed to the heights of Mount Sinai by angels. She became the patron saint of virgins, particularly those in search of husbands, and it was the custom until the late 19th century for the young women of Abbotsbury to go to the chapel and invoke her aid. They would put a knee in one of the wishing holes in the south doorway, their hands in the other two holes, and make a wish.

As the chapel overlooks the sea, it is likely to have been used as a beacon or sea-mark after the Dissolution,

The south face of the chapel

which may have ensured its preservation. In later times a navigation light was kept burning at the top of its stair turret.

Description

Although no records survive of its building, the chapel can be dated in style to the late 14th century. It is a sturdy rectangular structure, built entirely of the local golden buff limestone. The walls are high and heavily buttressed to take the stone vaulted roof; rainwater drains off the roof through holes in the parapet wall between the buttresses. At the north-east corner a stair turret, octagonal on the outside, rises above the roof and gives access to the parapet. It also contains a tiny oratory at roof level. Originally the buttresses and the stair turret were crowned with pinnacles. There are porches on both north and south walls.

The overall effect of the chapel is of a structure far larger than it actually is. The high walls and tall parapets are designed to impress, while the sense of grandeur is further enhanced by the chapel's lofty position.

Inside, the effect in medieval times would have been just as rich, with stained glass in the windows, and details of the roof picked out in bright colours. At the intersections of the vaulting are bosses carved with foliage, figure subjects and animals. A large triple window lights the east wall, and there are smaller windows on the other walls.

The walk up to the chapel provides excellent views down over Abbotsbury village and the abbey site.

½ mile S of Abbotsbury by path from village off B3157; the path leads off the lane to the Swannery (signposted) *OS Map 194; ref SY 573848*

Christianity became widely established in Britain after it was adopted as the official religion of the Roman Empire in the 4th century AD. Since that time it appears to have had a continuous existence in the South West, and when the Christian Saxon King Ine of Wessex conquered Somerset in the 7th century he found a community of monks already established there. It was probably Ine who founded Muchelney Abbey in 693, and he also provided the money for the first stone church to be built at Glastonbury in 712. During most of the Anglo-Saxon period the Old English church was inspired and led by monks, in the work of conversion, as well as building new monasteries, cathedrals and churches.

It was Glastonbury that led the great revival of English monasticism in the 10th century, after the Danish invasions of the 9th century had all but wiped out English monasteries and badly damaged church organisation. Abbot Dunstan, a Somerset monk of noble family and later archbishop of Canterbury, restored a community of Benedictine monks to Glastonbury in 943; in 967 Edmund, king of Wessex was buried there and in 1016 Edmund Ironside too, cementing Glastonbury's position as an important centre of pilgrimage. Throughout the Middle Ages it remained the wealthiest monastery in England.

Monasticism did not remain unchanged during the medieval period. The reforming monastic orders of the 12th century

Above left: The south cloister walk at Muchelney Abbey
Below: The remains of Glastonbury Abbey

wanted to return to a purer, more rigorous form of monastic life. The most successful in England were the Cistercians, whose rapid expansion during the 12th century is one of the most dramatic features of monastic history. They emphasised the importance of poverty, simplicity and hard work and established their houses in remote places – the location of Cleeve Abbey in Somerset is typically isolated. The order that perhaps most directly owes its origins to the west country is that of the Carthusians, whose monks lived almost as hermits: their first English house was established in 1179 by Henry II at Witham, near Frome in Somerset, as part of his penance for the murder of Thomas Becket.

After the Black Death of 1348 there was a decline in the population of monks, and almost no new monasteries were built. In the South West as elsewhere the mendicant orders, or friars, gained popularity at the expenses of the monasteries in the 14th century: in contrast to the earlier religious orders, the friars saw their task as taking the word of God to the people, and their more personal religious teaching proved a great success.

The isolated setting of Cleeve Abbey is typical of the locations the Cistercians chose for their monasteries

The power of monastic houses in the South West gave rise to some bitter quarrels between monks and townspeople in the Middle Ages. In Sherborne, for example, in 1437, the townspeople set fire to the abbey after a long-running quarrel over minor grievances. Such disputes may in part explain why there was so little lay resistance to the Dissolution of the Monasteries in the 1530s. After the Dissolution, most monasteries in the South West were destroyed or left to fall into ruin: only a handful, such as Christchurch in Dorset, survived to serve as parish churches after the monks had gone.

The motte and keep

The arms of the de Redvers

History

Christchurch has a typical motte-and-bailey castle, dating back to the early 12th century. Its chamber block, set on a river bank, is an unusually early surviving example of grand domestic architecture in England.

Duke William of Normandy's victory at Hastings in 1066 was decisive in more ways than one: not only were his Saxon enemies defeated, but they were soon deprived of almost all their lands. Chroniclers were surprised at the lack of serious resistance and one attributed it to the absence of castles in England. Within a generation all this had changed: as the Norman barons spread out through England, they built castles at every important location. Some lasted only a few years; others grew into the administrative centres of powerful earldoms.

Christchurch was a rich and important port in the 11th century. In 1100 Henry I granted the manor of Christchurch, then known as Twineham, to his cousin, Richard de Redvers, who had supported him against his brother Robert. It was probably Richard who built the great earthen mound or motte, the earliest feature of the castle, which would have been topped with a timber tower. His son, Baldwin, became first Earl of Devon, but it was Baldwin's brother, Richard, the second Earl (1155–62), who rebuilt the castle in stone, and erected the great chamber block – the so-called Norman House, or Constable's House – across the courtyard, against the curtain wall.

After the death of Earl Richard's son, Baldwin, in 1180, the castle continued in the family of the earls of Devon until 1293 when, on the death of Isabella de Fortibus, sister of the seventh Earl, it passed to the Crown. It was granted at various times to different noble families, and although its military role was at an end the Norman House continued as the residence of the constable responsible for the security of the buildings. Its defences were dismantled by order of Parliament in 1651, even though it had played little part in the Civil War. Local people helped themselves to the building materials, and by the late 17th century the castle was a ruin.

A corbel (stone support) in the parish church, possibly depicting Isabella de Fortibus

Christchurch priory, castle and town as they might have appeared in the late 12th century, by Ivan Lapper. The defended courtyard or bailey between the castle mound and the river contained many buildings, of which only the Normman House (bottom left) now survives

41

Description

The only remains of the castle now to be seen above ground are those of the chamber block or Norman House, on the east side of the former bailey, and the keep standing on the mound or motte. As the name implies, the Norman House was a domestic building. Roofless though it is, it provides a clear indication of the high level of accommodation which a baron of first rank had come to expect by the late 12th century. The main rooms were on the first floor: an external staircase led to a doorway in the side of the building facing the keep.

Passing through the entrance, a visitor would have found himself in a narrow lobby. Doors on the left led into a large hall, open to the roof and lit by handsome two-light windows. As these are raised above the ground they are larger than the narrow slits of the floor below, and are widely splayed to let in as much light as possible. The fine north window, being at the upper or high-table end of the hall, is especially elaborate. To the right of the lobby was a private chamber or solar: this room had an adjoining latrine built out over a millstream of the River Avon, which flows by the building on the other side. The east or river wall is thicker than the others, for it also served as the curtain wall of the castle. It probably had battlements and a

The chamber block or Norman House

wall-walk. Its chief feature is its tall, circular Norman chimney.

A bowling green, occupying the site of the castle bailey, now separates the Norman House from the castle motte, from the top of which there is a good view of the whole area. The motte, 9m (30 ft) high, is crowned by an unusually shaped keep: oblong in plan with splayed angles, internally it is 10m (33 ft) long by 9m (30 ft) wide, with 3m (10 ft) thick walls. It seems to have been at least three storeys high, with the entrance probably at first-floor level. The style of the keep, with chamfered angles in place of the flat corner buttresses usual in a 12th-century rectangular keep, suggests that it was probably built after 1300; the motte seems to have been enlarged to its present size to accommodate it.

Town, castle and parish church form a remarkably complete ensemble at Christchurch. The parish (once the priory) church, said to be the longest in England, was refounded as an Augustinian priory in

1150, from which the town takes its name. It has a magnificent 15th-century choir opening out beyond the Norman nave, and a 14th-century reredos (the screen behind the high altar), the only one in England to retain some of its original figure sculpture. The church is well known also for its holy beam: cut too short during the 12th-century rebuilding, it was found to have miraculously lengthened overnight, giving rise to the story that Christ had been among the carpenters working on the church.

A cutaway view of the Norman House, by Ivan Lapper, looking from the private chamber into the hall

In Christchurch town centre, near the priory church
OS Map 195; ref SZ 160927

Fiddleford Manor from the south-east

Opposite: *The solar. You can see traces of wall-painting on the far wall*

History

Fiddleford is a medieval manor house, completed in about 1370. It has undergone many changes since, but the splendid timber roofs over the great hall and solar are said to be the most spectacular in Dorset. They reflect the original owner's rising status and ambition: in the 14th century it was essential for a great man to entertain lavishly, and these rooms represent just the kind of conspicuous expenditure that would be expected of a man of authority and means.

The manor house has no recorded history, but it was probably built for William Latimer, sheriff of Somerset and Dorset. Men like Latimer, as sheriffs and justices, made the king's government work in the shires – a practical alliance between central authority and local influence. Latimer had acquired the Fiddleford estate by marrying the daughter of its previous owner, John Maury, in 1355. There must already have been a manor house here or close by, and a mill at Fiddleford is mentioned in the Domesday Book in 1086. However, Latimer clearly felt in need of a more up-to-date house to reflect his importance as a royal sheriff.

Description

The house is T-shaped, with Latimer's private residence contained in the two-storey cross-wing, to the left of the main south entrance door. This formed a comfortable house, with the service rooms (buttery and pantry) on the ground floor, and a large chamber (solar) above. Though much of the building has been altered, the original solar roof is complete. It is a magnificent oak structure, with graceful arched braces or trusses. There are traces of a wall-painting in the solar, where part of the Angel Gabriel from an Annunciation scene survives to hint at the richness of the original decoration.

To the right of the entrance is the two-storey great hall, essential for Latimer's duties as a royal official. Again the room has been much altered, but the elaborate roof, though incomplete and smoke-blackened, is still a fine sight with its elegantly arched and cusped struts and braces. The gallery at the west end above the screens or service passage is a 16th-century addition, and is now supported on a modern structure.

With its beautifully decorated walls, painted furniture, rush matting and fabric hangings beneath the great roofs, Latimer's

new house would have provided a statement of power that benefited both the king and his trusted agent, the new sheriff.

The house has undergone many alterations since Latimer's time. By the 16th century the house belonged to Thomas and Anne White, who extensively remodelled and enlarged it. Their initials feature on the 16th-century stone shields in the passage. In about 1660 the hall, which once extended almost to the river, was reduced in length by about 2m (6 ft); the present end-wall dates from that time, though the fireplace is a century older, having been moved from the south side of the hall. The north wing (still inhabited, and not open to the public) was added in the 16th century and the west wing, behind the solar, in the 18th century.

1 mile E of Sturminster Newton off A357; turn left for Fiddleford village, and entrance to the manor site is ¹/₄ mile from the main road (Please note that the adjoining building is a private residence and not open to visitors)
Open
1 Apr–30 Sep: daily 10am–6pm;
1 Oct–31 Mar: daily 10am–4pm
(closed 24–26 Dec and 1 Jan)
OS Map 194;
ref ST 801136

The remains of this Romano-Celtic temple, probably built during the 4th century AD, lie at the top of a hill on the South Dorset Downs, with fine views inland and out across Weymouth Bay.

When the armies of the Emperor Claudius invaded Britain in AD 43, the native population consisted of a number of British tribes. The southern tribes shared a common Celtic culture and were led by chieftains whose families may have formed a hereditary aristocracy, based in hillforts like Maiden Castle, 11km (7 miles) to the north of Weymouth.

The foundations of the temple

The Romans did not seek to disrupt this society. However, they set new standards of affluence and behaviour which the native nobility probably adopted as a sign of their status. The result was a version of the Roman way of life, with its roads, towns and country estates, adapted to the native culture.

The Jordan Hill site belongs to the end of the period of Roman occupation, when much of the economic structure was beginning to fragment, bringing changes to the social structure as well. It was apparently a small temple of a type common in Roman Britain: symmetrical in plan, with a central sanctuary or *cella* rising above a low columned portico which surrounded it on all four sides.

The temple was excavated in the 19th century and again in 1931, when the bases of four of the portico columns were located. The capital (head) and base of a fifth column were found loose near the north wall of the *cella*, and these can be seen in Dorchester Museum. Archaeologists found a well-like pit beneath the south-east corner of the sanctuary wall, about 4m (13 ft) deep and carefully lined with old roofing slabs. The pit contained 16 layers of ash and charcoal, alternating with layers of roofing slabs: between each of these were the bones of a bird and a small coin. At the bottom was a stone cist containing two urns, a sword and a spearhead. One of the coins dated from the reign of the Emperor Theodosius I (AD 379–95). Pits like this, used for ritual offerings, are a well-known feature of prehistoric Celtic religious sites throughout Europe, and suggest that many of the old pagan cults survived within the Roman Empire under a new guise, even after Christianity had become the official religion. Temples of this kind are known as Romano-Celtic because they appear to show a fusion of Celtic and classical religions.

Surrounding the temple was a large walled enclosure (not now accessible to visitors) about 30m (100 ft) square. Within this were found many animal bones and more 4th-century coins. To the north was a large cemetery where more than 80 skeletons were found, some originally in wooden coffins, others in stone cists. Many different personal objects were buried with thems, including pots, combs, jewellery, arrowheads and an iron sword. Some of these are now in Dorchester Museum. Clearly, some people wanted to be buried near these remote sites and believed in an afterlife associated with them, suggesting a well-organised rural community with powerful traditions. A separate hoard of over 4,000 bronze coins picked up near Jordan Hill in 1928 may represent offerings at the shrine collected over many years.

Foundations of a temple similar to that at Jordan Hill can be seen within the massive ramparts of the hillfort at Maiden Castle (see page 52). Other Roman remains nearby include a Romano-British villa at Preston, north of Jordan Hill, while there was a small Roman port to the west at Radipole, on the River Wey.

A coin from the reign of Emperor Theodosius I (AD 379–95)

2 miles NE of Weymouth, off A353 OS Map 194; ref SY 699821

47

The stone circle

The Kingston Russell circle is believed to date back to the later Neolithic or Early Bronze Age, some 4,000 years ago.

The building of great monuments, including stone circles, is one of the most fascinating aspects of later Neolithic Britain. The ability to construct such monuments flowed from a communications network that enabled resources from a wide area to be devoted to large scale projects: Avebury and Stonehenge are two of the best-known examples. Altogether

there are about 900 stone circles in the British Isles: of these, between 30 and 40 are found in the South West, mostly in Devon and Cornwall. Kingston Russell is one of only four in south Dorset, although the area is rich in other monuments of Neolithic and Bronze Age date. Stone circles were originally matched by elaborate circles of timber in parts of the country where this was the natural building material. In some places, stone circles appear to have been the permanent markers of former timber circles.

The 18 visible stones at Kingston Russell have all fallen: they lie flat, in a big irregular oval, the diameter of which varies between 27m (90 ft) and 18m (60 ft). Some are broken, and it is impossible to tell which fragments are bases and which were originally upper parts. Ploughing has also disturbed the site. None of the stones has been shaped in any way, but they may have been set up with the tallest to the north.

While we can never expect to know exactly what went on within such circles, the study of more recent primitive societies suggests that structures like this may have been put to a great variety of uses, such as religious ceremonies and calendar setting. They may have served as the setting for community decision-making, dynastic marriages, inter-community trading agreements and the settling of frontier disputes.

Back along the footpath towards the road you pass the remains of a much earlier Neolithic chambered tomb known as the Grey Mare and her Colts, showing that this area of chalk downland had been a focus for community ceremonies for at least one thousand years before the stone circle was erected.

Today, Kingston Russell Stone Circle lies at the junction of five footpaths, an echo of its ancient significance. It has a superb hilltop location, overlooking the village of Abbotsbury and the English channel, making it worth a visit just for the view.

Above: Two of the fallen stones
Below left: The nearby Neolithic long barrow known as the Grey Mare and her Colts

2 miles N of Abbotsbury; take minor road signposted to Hardy Monument from B3157 in Abbotsbury for 1¼ miles, then footpath for 1 mile
OS Map 194;
ref SY 578878

Not many parish churches stand in ruins, and fewer still occupy sites associated with prehistoric rituals. Four thousand years separate the main late Neolithic earthwork at Knowlton and the Norman church that stands at its centre. The earthwork itself is just one part of a landscape which is one of the great Neolithic and Bronze Age ceremonial complexes in southern England.

The main earthwork at Knowlton is of a type known as a henge. There are nearly one hundred henges in Britain and Ireland, dating from about 3000 to 2000 BC. Although they are generally believed to have been ceremonial sites, it is likely that they fulfilled many functions, and may have changed their role through time. Church Henge, as it is now known, has been protected from plough damage; the earthworks in the surrounding landscape have been less fortunate, but are still clearly visible in aerial photographs. There are three other main earthworks nearby: the Northern Circle and 'Old Churchyard' (both to the right of Church Henge in the photograph); and the Southern Circle, which encloses Knowlton Farm (top left), and is surrounded by a ditch 240m (790 ft) in diameter.

Associated with this group of henges is one of the greatest concentrations of round barrows, or burial mounds, in Dorset. The clump of trees 60m (200 ft) to the east of Church Henge marks the enormous Great Barrow, the largest individual barrow in the county. Many other barrows and ring-ditches survive

An aerial photograph of Knowlton earthworks seen from the north-east. The photograph was taken in 1995, when the dry weather revealed more earthworks

within a one-mile radius: stretching away to the north-west, for example, is the Dorset Cursus, twin banks of chalk about 2m (6 ft) high running for over 9km (6 miles), defining another zone in this ceremonial landscape. The high number and diversity of prehistoric and later archaeological remains surviving in this area of chalkland, known as Cranborne Chase, is partly due to the later history of the Chase as a royal hunting ground from at least Norman times, which meant that land use was strictly controlled.

The church was built in the 12th century and was in use until the 17th century, serving a now vanished hamlet by the riverside. Its Norman origins are evident from the plain round arch leading into the east end or chancel, and from the round-headed arches of the arcade dividing the nave from the

north aisle. The south door also looks Norman. The tower at the west end is 15th-century, and is built of flint with bands of stone; the line of the church roof is clearly visible on its eastern face. At the east end of the north aisle there appears to have been a lady chapel.

Whatever the reason for building a church within a Neolithic henge, the curious pairing has undoubtedly contributed to the survival of both, as an enduring symbol of the transition from pagan to Christian worship.

Above: A reconstruction painting of Church Henge at Knowlton as it might have appeared in Neolithic times, by Ivan Lapper

Left: The church

3 miles SW of Cranborne off B3078 OS Map 195; ref SU 024103

Maiden Castle is the largest and most complex Iron Age hillfort in Europe. Its massive banks, stretching across a saddle-backed hilltop 914m (3,000 ft) long, enclose an area the size of 50 football pitches. Excavations here in the 1930s and mid-1980s have shed much light on the development of the hilltop and the way of life of Iron Age communities in southern Britain. They have also yielded dramatic proof of British resistance to the Roman invasion in AD 43.

Early development

Though Maiden Castle as we see it today dates from the Iron Age (*c*800 BC – AD 43), the hillfort has much earlier origins. Like any complex fortress, it was not the product of one single phase of construction, but developed over a very long period.

The earliest evidence of occupation on the hilltop dates to about 6,000 years ago, when a small oval enclosure, surrounded by two lines of ditches, was built on the plateau at the eastern end of the site. This is now completely buried by the later earthworks and was only discovered by excavation. Around 3500 BC, after the enclosure had fallen out of use, a bank barrow – a mound 546m (1,790 ft) long, with ditches either side – was built, partly overlying the enclosure. This is just visible today as a low, curving earthwork running east–west across the hilltop. Its shape

Maiden Castle from the south-east

and size suggest that it may have acted as a barrier or territorial divide rather than serving any ritual purpose.

The hilltop seems to have remained in use during the later Neolithic and Bronze Age periods, though probably on a reduced scale. Near the centre of the hillfort are two burial mounds of a type known as bowl barrows, one of them about 20m (48 ft) in diameter, which can be dated to this period.

The Iron Age hillfort

The Iron Age hillfort overlying the Neolithic enclosure took shape from about 400 BC, when a single large bank and two gateways were added. Between about 250 and 200 BC this fort was greatly extended to encompass the western knoll as well, more than doubling the original area and reaching its present extent of 19ha (47 acres). Later, during the mid-2nd century BC, extra ramparts were added and the inner rampart was heightened. The entrances to the fort became increasingly complex as more ramparts were added and the gateways redesigned.

This immense fort was probably the chief stronghold of a confederation known as the Durotriges, whose influence extended throughout Dorset and Somerset. The huge number of defended enclosures constructed

Maiden Castle as it might have looked in its final form, by Paul Birkbeck

53

during the Iron Age – 31 in Dorset alone – suggests long-term rivalry between different tribes. Maiden Castle may have developed more than others because it was well placed to exploit local resources.

The building of such a fort would have required not only a massive investment of labour but also great organisational strength. Excavations have revealed that it was home to several hundred people and their animals: the people lived in the large round huts typical of the Iron Age in Britain, and the interior would have been densely covered with houses, granaries, storage pits and other structures, including paved roads.

During the later Iron Age major changes appear to have taken place on the hilltop. The number of people living here declined

dramatically, and occupation became restricted to the eastern half of the fort. The street system and internal organisation that were features of the hillfort around 100 BC seem to have been abandoned, and the defences became less important to the inhabitants: some of the outer ditches at the eastern entrance were filled in, and settlement and industrial activity extended into the area in front of the eastern gateway. It was this rather reduced hillfort that faced the invading Romans in AD 43.

Roman invasion and after

Maiden Castle was almost certainly one of 20 *oppida* (towns) taken by the 2nd Augusta legion during their successful campaign against the Durotriges under the future emperor Vespasian, in AD 43. Excavation of a small cemetery of about 30 burials near the eastern gateway provided vivid evidence of Maiden Castle's dramatic fall: one of those buried there had been killed by a Roman ballista bolt, found embedded in his backbone.

A reconstruction of later Iron Age houses in the south-west corner of the hillfort, by Miranda Schofield

54

Others bore the traces of sword cuts – some had been struck several times. However, the defenders' slings, their normal weapons, must have done much damage too. Large hoards of unused slingstones – one comprising as many as 20,000 selected beach pebbles – were uncovered by excavation.

Maiden Castle proved no match for the superior equipment and professionalism of the Roman army. The tribal rivalries that may have spurred the development of hillforts may also have been the cause of their downfall when faced with the full shock of the Roman assault. Writing about 50 years after the Roman invasion of Britain, the Roman historian Tacitus gave his reasons for the Britons' defeat: 'nothing has helped us more in fighting against this powerful nation than their inability to co-operate'.

By the end of the 1st century AD Maiden Castle had been abandoned, and the Roman town of Durnovaria (Dorchester) had been established to the north-east as the regional capital. However, late in the 4th century the Romanised inhabitants of the new town built a small temple, with a priest's house attached to it, within the north-east quarter of the deserted ramparts, and this seems to have remained in use for several centuries. The foundations of the temple and house now form the only visible structure within the hillfort.

Today, the dramatic threefold defences still dominate the landscape. As Thomas Hardy wrote in 1913: 'The profile of the whole stupendous ruin, as seen at a distance of a mile eastwards, is clearly cut as that of a marble inlay. … It may indeed be likened to an enormous many-limbed organism of an antediluvian time … lying lifeless, and covered with a thin green cloth, which hides its substance, while revealing its contour.' Standing at the foot of the highest ramparts and looking up, you can still appreciate the formidable obstacle that the defences presented to any attacker.

A bronze statue of the goddess Minerva, excavated from the Roman temple and now in Dorset County Museum

2 miles S of Dorchester; access off A354 Dorchester–Weymouth, N of bypass
OS Map 194; ref SY 669884

The counties of the South West have been the birthplace and inspiration of many artists and writers, and enjoy special associations with the Romantic poets. Samuel Taylor Coleridge was born in Ottery St Mary, Devon in 1772, and spent his most productive time living at Nether Stowey near Bridgwater in Somerset in the 1790s. When William Wordsworth and his sister Dorothy moved into nearby Alfoxden House, the two poets collaborated on the groundbreaking *Lyrical Ballads* (1798) which featured Coleridge's 'Rime of the Ancient Mariner' and

Wordsworth's 'Tintern Abbey'. The poem 'Kubla Khan' famously came to Coleridge in a reverie, but while setting it to paper he was interrupted by a 'person on business from Porlock' (on the Somerset coast) and was subsequently unable to recall the remaining lines.

The River Frome and Avon Gorge provided favoured subjects for Irish painter Francis Danby (1793–1861), a member of the 18th-century Bristol School. Plymouth was the birthplace of the painter Cecil Collins in 1908, and during his residence in Totnes in the 1930s and 1940s many of his paintings of dreamlike landscapes, angels and fools were exhibited at Dartington Hall. The artist Beryl Cook settled in Plymouth in the 1960s, and her time as a seafront landlady there doubtless provided inspiration for her humorous depictions of plump middle-aged bathing belles.

Above: *Samuel Taylor Coleridge in 1804, after a painting by James Northcote*

Left: *The Avon Gorge from beneath the Sea Walls, 1820, by Francis Danby*

The landscape of Devon was powerfully evoked in Henry Williamson's ecological novel *Tarka the Otter*, published in 1928. Williamson had settled in Georgeham on returning from the First World War and set his tale between the Rivers Taw and Torridge. Resident poet Alice Oswald celebrates another Devon river in her remarkable book-length poem *Dart* (2002). The moorland around Malmsmead and Oare in Exmoor is famously featured in R. D. Blackmore's *Lorna Doone*, published in 1869.

It was the human scene that provided a rich seam of literary material for Jane Austen, who lived in Bath for five years from 1801 and set *Northanger Abbey* and many chapters of *Persuasion* there. She also used the famous Cobb, the curving breakwater at Lyme Regis, Dorset, as the setting for Louisa Musgrove's dramatic fall in *Persuasion*, one of the crucial moments of the novel.

Dorset is above all the county of Thomas Hardy. He was born in 1840 at Higher Bockhampton on the edge of Egdon Heath, the backdrop to many of his Wessex novels. In 1885 he built Max Gate, a substantial red-brick villa south-east of Dorchester, where he spent the remaining 43 years of his life.

Among Hardy's many literary visitors was T. E. Lawrence, better known as Lawrence of Arabia. He rented and later bought Clouds Hill, a house near Bovington, as a retreat, and it was here that he wrote *The Seven Pillars of Wisdom* in 1926. He was on his way to meet Henry Williamson when he was killed in a motorbike accident in 1935. Eric Kennington's marble effigy of his friend in Arab dress can be seen in St Martin's Church, Wareham.

Thomas Hardy (left) and his wife, Emma, at Max Gate, c1900

Lying in a wooded glade just yards from the busy A35, this little stone circle resembles a huddle of ancient conspirators, lurking in the trees.

The Nine Stones, which are very irregular in shape and size, are arranged in a near circle, which has a maximum diameter of 8m (26 ft). Seven of the stones are under 1m (3 ft) high, although as they are all partially buried they may be larger than the exposed parts suggest. Two larger stones on the north-west side of the circle are about 1.5m (5 ft) high and 1.5m wide. The stones are roughly spaced at 1m intervals around the circle, though there is a gap of 3m (10 ft) between the two larger stones suggesting a possible entrance.

Stone circles are found throughout England. They are concentrated in upland areas such as Bodmin Moor, Dartmoor and the Lake District, although this may not reflect their original distribution. Where excavated, they have been found to date from the Late Neolithic to Middle Bronze Age (*c*2500–1000 BC).

Opposite: Part of the stone circle

Left: One of the Nine Stones

All are carefully laid out, with the stones regularly spaced. Although we do not fully understand why they were built or how they were used, it is clear that they had ritual importance for the people who used them: in many cases, excavation has revealed evidence of burials and associated rituals. Some seem to have been carefully aligned so as to help mark the passage of time and the seasons.

The Nine Stones is one of only four stone circles to survive in south Dorset, and its location in a valley bottom is very unusual.

½ mile W of Winterbourne Abbas on A35 (park in layby opposite, N of road, and cross road with care)
OS Map 194; ref SY 611904

59

The motorist driving along the A35 has scarcely a moment to take in this group of barrows, or burial mounds, straddling the road west of Winterbourne Abbas. These belong to one of several Bronze Age cemeteries in the area, which has the highest density of Bronze Age barrows anywhere in the world. In this particular cemetery alone there are 44 barrows, dating from about 1500 BC.

Barrows are traditionally classified according to their shape. Long barrows date from the time of the

Some of the barrows forming part of the Bronze Age cemetery

earliest farmers: some of them, like West Kennet in Wiltshire, are very large, containing several burial chambers, and remained in use for hundreds of years. Round barrows, the kind found at Winterbourne, date from the Late Neolithic or Early Bronze Age, and are usually divided into four types: bowl (steep-sided); bell (where the mound is separated from a surrounding ditch by a narrow platform); disc (flatter, with a wider ditch); and pond (hollow in the middle and surrounded by a bank). However, it is now realised that the present eroded shape of these burial mounds may give little clue to their original appearance thousands of years ago.

All four types of round barrow can be found at Winterbourne, including the rarer disc and pond barrows. Some are in groups of two or three, perhaps suggesting family relationships. The largest barrow is a bowl barrow, at the centre of the group: it has a diameter of 35m (115 ft) and is 2.5m (8 ft) high. To the west of this is a large group comprising one disc

An aerial view of the Poor Lot Barrows, looking south

barrow and seven bowl barrows.

Very few of the barrows here have been excavated, and we do not know what kind of burials they contain. Some may contain bodies, although by the Early Bronze Age cremation had become common: the ashes of the dead were placed in pots with a raised band around the top, known as collared urns. Sometimes food vessels are found with the urn, and occasionally weapons such as bronze daggers or stone axe heads.

Unusually, the Poor Lot Barrows are located across the bottom and sides of a valley, rather than on a ridge or hilltop as was the norm.

2 miles W of Winterbourne Abbas, S of junction of A35 with minor road to Compton Valence. Access via Wellbottom Lodge, 180m (200 yds) along A35 E of junction OS Map 194; ref SY 590907

SOMERSET

The landscape of the historic county of Somerset – now divided into Somerset, Bath and North East Somerset, and North Somerset – bears witness to human habitation from earliest times. The mysterious stone circles at Stanton Drew and the long barrow at Stoney Littleton are important religious sites that were in use over 4,000 years ago.

Water is an important element of the Somerset landscape. The drained fenlands of the Somerset Levels have been reclaimed from the sea and bog over thousands of years, and lake villages developed here as early as the Iron Age. From the medieval lakeside village of Meare, the 14th-century fish house provided a plentiful food supply for the monks of Glastonbury Abbey.

The moorland plateau of Exmoor straddles the Devon–Somerset border and ends abruptly at the Bristol Channel, forming England's highest coastline. On its eastern fringes, the town of Dunster flourished as a market for cloth in the Middle Ages, when Exmoor was an important centre of the woollen industry.

Sir Bevil Grenville's Monument, near Lansdown, commemorates the fall of a Royalist commander during the dark days of the Civil War. Some 40 years later the last battle to take place on English soil – the battle of Sedgemoor, which saw the defeat of Monmouth's rebellion against James II – was fought in this county, on 7 July 1685.

Left: Engine house in the Brendon Hills
Opposite: An Exmoor landscape, west of Porlock

Sir Bevil Grenville's Monument

Dunster:
Gallox Bridge,
Yarn Market
& Butter Cross

Stanton Drew Circles & Cove

Stoney Littleton Long Barrow

Farleigh Hungerford Castle

Nunney Castle

Meare Fish House

Cleeve Abbey

Glastonbury
Tribunal

Muchelney Abbey

Gallox Bridge

and monuments: three of these are in the care of English Heritage and shed light on the period of Dunster's prosperity.

GALLOX BRIDGE

In the Middle Ages wool was England's chief export, and the source of much of the country's wealth. Taxes on wool exports paid for Edward I's conquest of Wales and his near conquest of Scotland. At this time Dunster flourished as a market and port for wool, fleeces being brought down from the moor to be sold there. Many of them were carried by packhorse across the River Avill via Gallox Bridge, originally the main route into Dunster from the south. The original name of the bridge was Doddebrigge, by which it is referred to in the 14th century, but by Tudor times it had become Gallocksbrigge, Gallox Bridge, or Gallocks Bridge. All these names derive from

Lying between the wooded hills of Exmoor and the sea, Dunster is one of the most attractive villages in Somerset. In the 12th century it sat on the coast, and thrived as the main trading port for Exmoor; when the sea retreated, leaving Dunster 2 miles inland, it continued to prosper as a centre of the wool trade. Today Dunster is a popular visitor attraction, and retains many fine historic buildings

A sheep pen, from the 14th-century Luttrell Psalter

the gallows that stood on a hill outside the village. The gallows were a symbol of the authority of the lords of Dunster Castle, who had the right to try and hang any thief caught within the area of their jurisdiction.

The bridge is 1.2m (4 ft) wide and 10.5m (32 ft) long, and has two slightly pointed arches. Each side has four narrow chamfered ribs. On the village side, the bridge parapet is continued along the footpath for some way beside the river, in order to prevent flooding. Alongside the bridge is an ancient ford for wheeled traffic. The bridge is still in use as a public footbridge, and is an integral part of the medieval landscape of Dunster.

YARN MARKET

By the 16th and 17th centuries demand had shifted from raw wool to finished cloth. Since Dunster cloth was woven in nearby mills, the village remained prosperous, as the building of the Yarn Market shows. Built in 1609 and repaired in 1647, it sits in the middle of the high street as a monument to this trade. Before it was built, most of the buying and selling would have been done in the open air, but the English weather being what it is there must have been occasions when trading was halted by wind or rain; sellers must also have been worried about the security of their goods. The Yarn Market was a permanent solution to all these problems.

The Yarn Market

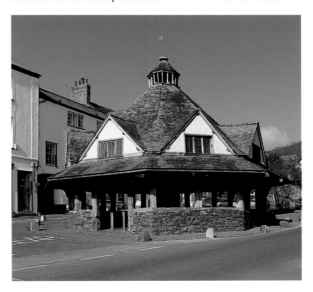

Opposite: The Butter Cross

An engraving of the Yarn Market in 1821, with the castle beyond

The building is octagonal in shape, and built almost entirely of wood. Gables over each side contain windows which help to light the interior; a central stone pillar topped by a bell turret supports the open roof. The different parts of the building make up a harmonious whole; note how the eaves were made to project in order to give shelter to prospective customers as they inspected the goods laid out for sale.

BUTTER CROSS

Outside the village on the Alcombe road is the Butter Cross, which probably once stood at the north end of the high street. Although now relegated to a bank beside a minor road out of the village, the cross has an important story to tell. In the Middle Ages the symbolism of the cross was everywhere: a Victorian antiquarian listed over 200 outdoor crosses in Somerset alone, linking them with Glastonbury as an early missionary centre. Crosses acted as boundaries and as memorials: Edward I (reigned 1272–1307) erected a series of beautiful and elaborate crosses to mark the resting places of the coffin of his wife, Eleanor, on its way from Lincoln, near where she died, to Westminster Abbey where she is buried. At the time of the

Reformation, crosses became a symbol of superstition, and many were destroyed or moved.

Like the Dunster Butter Cross, many crosses stood in the centre of towns and villages and naturally became places where merchants would strike deals. The Butter Cross probably acquired its name from the fact that butter was sold near its original site. It is not known when it was removed to its present location, though local tradition says this was in 1825. The head of the cross has disappeared, but the broken shaft seems to date from the 15th century. If so, it was probably the last of several replacements.

Dunster has much else to offer the visitor. A good place to start is at the Exmoor National Park Visitor Centre, which tells the story of the wool trade centred on Dunster. The priory church is mostly 15th-century but is Norman in origin, and contains the tombs of the Luttrell family, owners of Dunster Castle, and a fine rood screen. The monastic tithe barn and circular 13th-century dovecote stand near the church, and fragments of another medieval cross can be found in the churchyard near the west door. Dunster Castle sits on a hill at the edge of the village: first built as a motte-and-bailey castle in the years following the Norman Conquest, it was extensively refortified in the 13th century and modernised in the late 17th century. Remodelling in the 19th century gave the castle its present romantic, embattled skyline. Now in the care of the National Trust, it was owned by the Luttrell family for 600 years.

Dunster is 2 miles E of Minehead. Large car park by visitor centre.
Yarn Market: in High St
OS Map 181;
ref SS 992438
Gallox Bridge: at S end of village; from car park walk along High St, turning right along West St then left down Park St (signposted)
OS Map 181;
ref SS 989432
Butter Cross: On minor road to Alcombe; take footpath just beyond the visitor centre on the right
OS Map 181;
ref SS 988439

WATERLOGGED HERITAGE:

The Somerset Levels are a unique and beautiful area of the British Isles. They consist of low-lying peat moors interrupted by islands of sand and rock – most of the area is no more than 8m (25 ft) above sea-level. Not only is it one of the most important wetland areas in terms of wildlife, in which it is immensely rich, but it also provides a unique archaeological record within its layers of waterlogged peat.

The Levels were probably completely submerged until around 4500 BC, when peat deposits began to form. Remarkable evidence for the occupation of the Levels in the Neolithic period survives in the form of the wooden trackways that crossed the Levels in many places, linking areas of higher ground over the peat bogs. These have survived exceptionally well in the waterlogged ground, but are now in danger of drying out due to the effects of modern commercial peat cutting – the same

A reconstructed length of the Sweet Track

activity that revealed them. The trackways were constructed from planks, poles or rails, secured by pegs or other timbers. The oldest known is the Sweet Track (named after the peat-cutter who discovered it) which has been dated to 3806 BC. The amount of timber used – 4,000m (13,000 ft) of plank, 2,000m (6,500 ft) of heavy rails and 6,000 pegs – which all had to be felled, split and prepared before construction began, suggests an organised community with considerable resources of manpower.

During the Iron Age, around 400 BC, two major settlements were established on the Levels: the famous Lake Villages of Glastonbury and Meare. The Glastonbury settlement was sited in an area where open water predominated. It was built on a great platform of felled timber incorporating a landing stage and a palisade, inside which were many buildings. These were circular structures with a thick clay floor, vertical wattle and daub walls and a raised hearth. In contrast, the settlement at Meare may have been more like a seasonal trading centre – there is no palisade and there may not have been any permanent dwellings. The inhabitants of both these villages were

Excavations at Glastonbury Lake Village in the early 19th century

farmers, keeping animals, growing crops and using the abundant natural resources around them. They were also sophisticated craftsmen, as the many remains of decorated pottery ('Glastonbury style') and artefacts such as glass beads attest.

By medieval times, the ecclesiastical estates of Glastonbury, Wells and Muchelney owned large parts of the area, which they began to enclose and to protect from flooding through the construction of floodbanks such as Burrow Wall. The courses of rivers running through the Levels, such as the Brue, were straightened to improve drainage. The area was an important source of food for the monasteries. The abbot of Glastonbury's fish house still stands at Meare, where there was a large lake in the Middle Ages (see page 72).

From 1770 to 1840 the land was enclosed and many rhynes (ditches) were cut, draining and dividing the land into the rectangular units that we can see today in the pattern of roads and farms. The balance between drainage and maintenance of the wetland water levels is, however, a delicate one. Debate centres upon the need to retain the traditional landscape and conserve the soil, the water-logged monuments, and wildlife habitats, while at the same time protecting farming and its social fabric. English Heritage, in partnership with other bodies, is helping actively to promote initiatives that will help preserve this unique area for future generations.

Glastonbury Tor seen across the Levels

Glastonbury Tribunal

This fine late 15th-century town house, once thought to have been the courtroom of Glastonbury Abbey, now houses both the Tourist Information Centre and the Glastonbury Lake Village Museum, which contains dramatic finds from one of Europe's most famous archaeological sites.

Approaching Glastonbury today, it is hard to imagine the town dominated by the great abbey church, once as large as a cathedral; Glastonbury Abbey was one of the oldest and richest monastic communities in England. The house now known as

Glastonbury Tribunal owes its name to the fact that it was formerly mistakenly identified with the abbey's tribunals, where secular justice was administered in association with the management of the abbey's estates. However, it is possible that the house was used by one of the abbey's officials.

The building is a typical late medieval house, with a separate kitchen block at the rear. A passage leads from the front door through to the courtyard at the back. The present façade with its projecting first-floor bay was added in the early 16th century: the construction joints are clearly visible in the masonry. The Tudor rose and the badge of Abbot Beer (d. 1524) have been reset over the entrance to the passage.

Within the house, several internal partitions were added when the building was let to different tenants later in its history. The ground floor front room retains its arched fireplace with recesses on either side, and below the window the wooden panels, carved to imitate linen folds, date

SOMERSET

from the 16th century. Scars on the wall show the location of the medieval stairs, and corbels or supports mark the position of an upper floor. The room at the back was the main chamber and has a fine panelled ceiling; the four-light window in the north wall is original, while those in the east and west walls were inserted in the 17th century. The kitchen block at the back of the house is a separate building added in Elizabethan times.

The first floor, which now houses the Lake Village Museum, repeats the arrangement of the ground floor. The main room at the front extends over the entrance passage and retains its fine original open roof.

Glastonbury Lake Village Museum

Two thousand years ago much of Somerset's landscape was covered by marshy sea, and settlers were drawn

Detail of a corbel from the rear of the building

to the island refuge provided by Glastonbury's famous tor. Although the marshes have long since been drained, the peaty soil acts as a good preservative. In 1892 an amateur archaeologist discovered a number of earth mounds near the road between Glastonbury and Godney, just to the north. These proved to be the remains of an Iron Age village built on an artificial platform around 1.4ha (3.5 acres) in extent, reached by dug-out canoe and by a network of wooden trackways laid across the marshland.

Hundreds of artefacts were recovered from the site, including many items made of wood, iron and bronze. The Glastonbury Lake Village Museum, on the upper floor of Glastonbury Tribunal, displays some of the finds which illustrate the domestic, craft and industrial activities of the occupants.

9 High St, Glastonbury
Please phone
01458 832954
for opening times
or visit www.
glastonburytic.co.uk
(There is an admission charge for the Museum)
OS Map 182; ref ST 499389

71

History

The 14th-century fish house at Meare is believed to be the only survival in England of a building constructed to serve the needs of a medieval monastic fishery.

As head of one of the richest monasteries in England, the abbot of Glastonbury played host to the most powerful men in the land, including the king, and on such occasions the menu might include many types of fish, especially pike and carp. Nearly every monastery had its fish pond, but the abbot of Glastonbury's lake at Meare exceeded them all in size. Although the fish house stands today in the middle of a field grazed by cows, in late medieval times the lake would have stretched northwards from the line of the present river bank into the far distance. Five miles in circumference and nearly 200ha (500 acres) in area, it was a valuable resource which the abbey guarded jealously.

This small house was most probably constructed by Abbot Adam of Sodbury (1322–35) close to the manor house he used as a summer retreat. It was built for the abbot's water bailiff, the official charged with keeping watch over the lake. The abbey was dissolved in 1539 and the lake drained 200 years ago, but the fish house survives well, although it was quite badly damaged in a fire at the end of the last century.

Description

The fish house was originally planned as a two-storey building with a first-floor hall and smaller rooms on the

Meare Fish House

ground floor, which did not interconnect with the rooms above. You can see traces on the wall of an external staircase which led up to the former entrance on the first floor, together with a

The abbey's servants probably fished from boats using nets, as illustrated in this 14th-century English manuscript

chimney stack beside it. On the north-west corner there was also a small two-storey extension, which was probably a latrine tower.

Inside, there were three (possibly four) rooms on the ground floor in which fish could be dried, salted and stored for use in winter. The upper floor was divided into a hall and bedroom; a door in the corner of the bedroom opened into a now vanished latrine. Note the corbels that supported the vanished floor joists. At the east end of the hall is a fine two-light window: the wave form of the pointed arches above is a hallmark of the Decorated style of Gothic. This detail, and the hall fireplace, reveal that despite its modest purpose the

building was richly finished. Glastonbury Abbey's water bailiff enjoyed a higher standard of living than many of his contemporaries, and certainly better than that of the poachers he was doubtless expected to catch.

Across the field from the fish house lie the parish church and Manor Court Farm, now a private residence, which is all that remains of Abbot Adam's summer retreat. In its original form it was probably twice as large. A weathered statue of an abbot crowns the gable of the porch. The church has a medieval pulpit and alms box; the chancel roof is an almost exact copy of the original roof of the fish house.

In Meare village on B3151. Open at any reasonable time: key to the interior available from Manor Court Farm, next door to church
OS Map 182; ref ST 458417

74

NUNNEY CASTLE

History

Built by a soldier returned from the wars, Nunney is as much the realisation of an ideal as a stronghold intended for serious defence. When completed in the late 14th century it would have looked more like an illumination in a contemporary manuscript than a typical English castle.

Sir John de la Mare spent much of his life fighting with the Black Prince, Edward III's eldest son, in south-west France. Like the knight in Chaucer's *Canterbury Tales* he did well out of the wars, collecting enough ransoms and plunder to ensure a comfortable and secure old age. He obtained a licence to fortify his manor house at Nunney from Edward III in 1373, and then proceeded to build something distinctly un-English – in fact, his rebuilding seems to have been inspired by the style of architecture he was used to seeing on campaign in France.

Nunney's highly distinctive design was not taken up by any imitators in England. Although effective cannon were beginning to make their appearance when Nunney was built, the castle has no gunports: it represents the final stage in the pre-artillery era of castle building, and style rather than defensive strength seems to have been the main influence in its design.

This late 15th-century French illustration of a siege shows a castle of the type that probably inspired Nunney

The interior of the castle was remodelled in the late 16th century.

During the Civil War between king and Parliament in the mid-17th century, a Colonel Prater attempted to hold Nunney for the king against Parliamentarian forces. His small garrison managed to hold out for only two days in 1645 before surrendering the castle after the north wall of the tower was severely damaged by gunfire. This wall eventually collapsed in 1910.

Description

What remains of John de la Mare's castle today is a tall, four-storey rectangular building with large,

Opposite: The castle from the south-east

equally sized round towers at each corner. On the short sides these are only 1m (3 ft) apart, whereas on the long sides the connecting walls are some 12m (38 ft) long. Seventeenth-century drawings show that the corner towers were once surmounted with high conical roofs, in the French fashion. The towers were joined

The north front of the castle

together by a single continuous fighting platform that encircled the entire castle at wall-walk level. This platform was carried on large projecting corbels, which are clearly visible – a feature seen in other castles of the period like Bodiam in Sussex and Scotney in Kent. Such fighting galleries were one of the

more important innovations in castle building of the period in France.

In his tower Sir John provided all the accommodation necessary for a comfortable aristocratic lifestyle. Within the shell of the castle, fireplaces, windows, doors and joist holes clearly mark the floor levels and suggest the original uses of each room. The lower two floors housed service rooms, including the kitchen on the ground floor, with a huge fireplace and the remains of a wall oven to one side. Lit only by narrow slits, these floors must always have been dark and gloomy. Over these was the great hall occupying most of the second floor, with a large fireplace, and there were additional chambers in the towers. The chambers on the third floor were reserved for the lord and his family; there was also a chapel in the south-west tower, indicated by a large mullioned window, and latrines occupied the north-east and south-east towers.

The quality of the masonry throughout is high, and you can see how the windows of the great hall and lord's apartments are more graceful and elaborate than those lower down; they also reveal the essentially non-defensive nature of the castle. Access to all the floors was via a large spiral staircase in the north-west tower.

The entrance, which was on the now ruined north side of the castle, was small and defended only by a drawbridge. The castle relied on its height and fighting platform to deter a would-be enemy. Beyond the moat, which encloses the building tightly,

there was a curtain wall on at least three sides of the castle, and there are traces of an outer bailey on the northern side. The site of the castle is very low, and despite the defence offered by the moat and the curtain wall, it is in a weak position, with rising ground nearby.

Nunney Castle remains dramatic and extremely picturesque, its setting enhanced by the moat and the adjoining early 18th-century Castle Farm. The church on the other side of the street from the castle contains monuments to the castle's founder and to its later owners, the Paulet and Prater families.

An engraving of the castle in 1733 by the Buck brothers

In Nunney,
3¹/₂ miles SW of
Frome off A361
*OS Map 183;
ref ST 737457*

Standing on the edge of Lansdown Hill, this early 18th-century monument commemorates the heroic death of the Royalist leader Sir Bevil Grenville at the battle of Lansdown in 1643.

When King Charles I raised his standard at Nottingham on 22 August 1642, he had no professional army at his command. In the first years of the Civil War troops on both sides were recruited in time-honoured fashion: the nobility and gentry called out their dependants and tenants to fight on whichever side their masters favoured. During the winter of 1642–3 four Cornish squires – Sir Bevil Grenville, Sir Nicholas Slanning, John Trevanion and John Arundel – raised a force of over 1,500 infantry that became the nucleus of the king's Western Army.

When fighting was renewed in spring 1643, the king prepared to attack London and dissolve the alienated Parliament. Under the command of Sir Ralph Hopton the Western Army marched north-eastwards from Devon while Charles moved south from Oxford. Hopton was opposed by an old comrade-in-arms, Sir William Waller, who commanded the Parliamentarian forces in the west country. Determined to prevent the two Royalist armies from joining together, Waller took up a strong position on

Sir Bevil Grenville's Monument

the top of Lansdown Hill near Bath, from which his guns could block the Royalist advance along the London road (now the A4).

On 5 July 1643 Grenville's Cornish infantry began fighting their way up the steep slopes to attack Waller's guns. It was an almost suicidal act of bravery. Twice the Cornish were beaten back, but the third time they reached and took the guns, fighting off a vigorous Parliamentarian counter-attack. It was in the course of this that Sir Bevil Grenville was killed. Even so, by nightfall the Royalists had won the battle; Waller retreated and the way was open for an attack on London.

At a time when many Englishmen still had doubts about the justice of the king's cause and his methods of government, Grenville's courage and the success of his Cornishmen had helped to inspire the Royalist war effort. The issues became much simpler on the battlefield – it was purely a matter of winning on the day. As William Cartwright put it, in the *Elegy on Sir Bevil Grenville* inscribed on the monument:

This was not Nature's courage, nor that thing
We valour call, which Time and Reason bring –
But a diviner fury, fierce and high,
Valour transported into Ecstasy.

Sir Bevil Grenville in 1636, engraved by Robert Cooper

It was Henry Grenville, Lord Lansdown, who erected the monument that now stands where his grandfather Sir Bevil died. Standing 7.6m (25 ft) high, it carries an inscription on the south side describing the battle and two poems on the north side, and is surmounted by a griffin bearing the Grenville coat of arms. As a piece of architecture, it is typical of the flamboyant style known as English Baroque.

Trees have now grown up around the monument, which would once have commanded a fine view over the valley below. It is difficult today to imagine the horror of the Civil War battle that took place on this spot.

4 miles NW of Bath on N edge of Lansdown Hill, near road to Wick (signposted) *OS Map 172; ref ST 722703*

The village of Stanton Drew preserves the third largest collection of standing stones in England. Yet, perhaps because it lies off the beaten track, its remarkable prehistoric stone circles have not received the same level of interest and exploration as the more famous examples at Avebury and Stonehenge. This obscurity, and the lack of modern intrusions into their surroundings, have protected their solitude and character. The great stones (or megaliths) and the patterns they make in the landscape remain mysterious: however, recent surveys carried out here have yielded dramatic results, and helped to clarify our understanding of the site.

Part of the Great Circle

There are three stone circles at Stanton Drew. The Great Circle, at 113m (370 ft) in diameter, is one of the largest in the country: it has 26 surviving upright stones, although there may once have been up to 30. The other two circles, to the south-west and north-east, are smaller. Both the Great Circle and the north-east circle were approached from the north-east by short 'avenues' of standing stones, most of which have fallen. In the garden of the village pub is a group of three large stones called The Cove, and to the north, across the River Chew, is the site of a standing stone known as Hautville's Quoit. Their closeness to each other, and the alignments between some of them, indicate that together these stones formed a single complex.

Stone circles like these are known to date broadly to the Late Neolithic and Early Bronze Age (c3000–2000 BC), and many examples are known. Such circles are believed to have played an important part in contemporary social and religious life, and there is evidence that some were aligned with major events of the solar and lunar calendar. However, they are difficult subjects to tackle archaeologically, and their interpretation is the subject of much discussion. In order to try to lift this veil of ignorance a little, in 1997 English Heritage initiated a geophysical survey of the large field

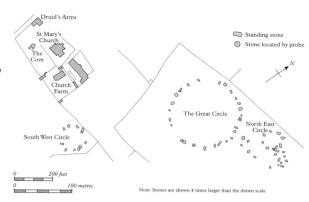

that contains the Great Circle and north-east circle. The survey used magnetometry, a non-invasive technique which picks up magnetic anomalies in the ground to indicate the presence of buried features such as pits, ditches and hearths.

The survey results were astonishing. At a stroke, they demonstrated that the remains at Stanton Drew are just the ruin of a much more elaborate and important site than had previously

Plan of the Circles and Cove

The Cove

been imagined. Lying under the pasture within the Great Circle are the remains of a complex pattern of buried pits, arranged in nine concentric rings within the stone circle, and further pits at the centre. It is difficult to make out individual features, but the pits seem to be about a metre or more across and spaced about a metre apart around the outer circle.

Just as remarkable was the discovery that the Great Circle is itself contained within a very large enclosure ditch, about 135m (440 ft) in diameter.

This interpretation by Peter Dunn of the wooden henge at Durrington Walls in Wiltshire gives some idea of how the wooden structures within the Great Circle at Stanton Drew might once have appeared

This is about 7m (23 ft) wide with a broad gap or entrance facing north-east. Such enclosures, or henges, are a well-known feature of later Neolithic Britain, and are assumed to have been centres of ritual activity. Several henges enclose stone circles, and some feature rings of pits. Sites that most resemble the patterns emerging at Stanton Drew include Woodhenge and Durrington Walls in Wiltshire: at these and other sites the pits are known to have held timber uprights, although it is not clear whether these were part of roofed or open structures. It seems likely that at least some of the pit circles at Stanton Drew once held massive posts. The circles are the largest and most numerous yet recorded at any site and surely indicate the investment of immense effort and enterprise in the service of prehistoric beliefs.

CHURCHMAN'S CIGARETTES

THE DANCERS OF STANTON DREW

The geophysical survey of the north-east stone circle found at its centre a quadrilateral of four pits aligned with the opposing pairs of the eight stones that comprise the circle. These may be ritual pits, or might perhaps be the holes for stones that have since been removed.

The circles were probably first noted by the famous antiquarian John Aubrey in 1664, and the first plan was published by William Stukeley in 1776. They remain very much as first recorded over 300 years ago. In the absence of many facts about them, the stones have attracted a rich tradition of folklore. The most persistent tale is that the stones are the petrified members of a wedding party and its musicians, lured by the Devil to celebrate on the Sabbath and thus being punished for their revels.

The legend associated with Stanton Drew, illustrated for Churchmans' 'Legends of Britain' series of cigarette cards, 1936

6 miles S of Bristol off B3130. Circles: E of Stanton Drew village; access at the discretion of the landowner, who may levy a charge. Cove: in garden of the Druid's Arms OS Map 172; Circles ref ST 601633; Cove ref ST 597631

Stoney Littleton Long Barrow

Stoney Littleton is a fine example of a chambered long barrow built during the Neolithic period (roughly 4000–2500 BC). Probably dating from *c*3500 BC, it is about 30m (100 ft) long, and features multiple side chambers in which human remains were once buried. The approach to the barrow – down a long narrow lane, across a stream and through fields – takes the visitor across a landscape that has probably been farmed continuously since Neolithic times.

Chambered long barrows mark an important stage in the evolution of prehistoric society in Britain. They seem to represent the emergence of élites among the early farming communities – élites whose status may have led them to develop ideas about ancestry and posterity that required impressive and durable structures for their expression. Although usually considered to have been tombs, it is possible that many long barrows were in fact shrines – places where the presence of the ancestral dead helped the living to contact their gods, much as a medieval church contains graves while being primarily intended for the living community that built it. Some barrows have provided evidence that use continued even after burials were no longer made.

The barrow at Stoney Littleton is considered one of the finest accessible examples of the 'true entrance' type of long barrow, where an entrance leads via a vestibule into a gallery or central passage with pairs of side chambers radiating from it. As is usual in long barrows, the entrance here is in the middle of the wider (south-east) end: the entrance portal is 1.1m (3 ft 9 in) high. Beyond the vestibule, the gallery is about 12.8m (42 ft) long, and varies between 1.2 and 1.8m (4–6 ft) high. It has dry stone walls with a frontage of upright slabs, and the roof consists of overlapping courses of stone converging to a final covering of small slabs. There are three sets of paired chambers, and a seventh chamber at the far end – the only known example of such an arrangement. In some later barrows the chambers open directly from the sides of the barrow, with the main entrance being a dummy, like the false doors in some Egyptian tombs.

Stoney Littleton has yielded very little evidence for the date of its construction or the number of people originally buried there. The barrow seems to have survived intact until about 1760, when the owner of the site, a local farmer, broke into the chambers in search of building stone; in the years that followed, most of the contents were stolen. The Revd John Skinner described some burnt bones and parts of two or three skeletons, which he found while excavating the barrow in 1816, but these have since been lost. A plaque beside the entrance records, rather smugly, that the restoration of the barrow in 1857 was carried out 'with scrupulous exactness'.

The barrow seen from the air

Left: *Plan of the long barrow*

1 mile S of Wellow off A367; car park by bridge over stream (short signposted walk uphill). You are advised to bring a torch
OS Map 172; ref ST 735572

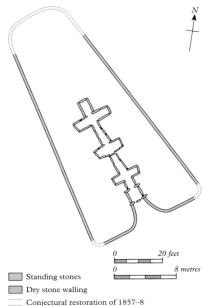

N

0   20 feet
0   8 metres

☐ Standing stones
☐ Dry stone walling
⋯ Conjectural restoration of 1857–8
⬭ Closing or septal slab

Eleven English Heritage sites in this area are staffed and most have a separate guidebook, which can be purchased at the site's gift shop or by mail order. These sites charge an admission fee, although admission is free to members of English Heritage (see inside back cover). Please note that sites listed here as opening on 1 April open at Easter if it falls earlier. Full details of admission charges, access and opening times for all of English Heritage's sites are given in the *English Heritage Members' and Visitors' Handbook* and on our website (www.english-heritage.org.uk).

Details of English Heritage publications can be found in the *Publications Catalogue*. To obtain a free copy of the catalogue, and to order English Heritage publications, please contact:

English Heritage Postal Sales
c/o Gillards, Trident Works
Temple Cloud, Bristol BS39 5AZ

Tel: 01761 452966 Fax: 01761 453408
email: ehsales@gillards.com

BERRY POMEROY CASTLE
DEVON

This romantic ruin, steeped in local folklore, lies in a picturesque Devon valley. Behind the grand gatehouse and defensive curtain wall of the late 15th-century castle are the remains of a flamboyant Elizabethan country house, built *c*1560–1600 by the powerful Seymour family. Edward Seymour, first Duke of Somerset, and uncle and governor of Edward VI, had acquired the castle in 1547.

Open 1 Apr–31 Oct. Please phone for admission prices and opening times: 01803 866618.

2¹/₂ miles E of Totnes off A385
OS Map 202; ref SX 839623

CLEEVE ABBEY
SOMERSET

Tucked away in a quiet part of Somerset, this is one of the few 13th-century monastic sites left with such a complete set of cloister buildings. It also has rare Cistercian wall paintings, a medieval painted chamber (viewing may be limited), magnificent timber ceiling and historically important tiled pavement.

Open 1 Apr–31 Oct. Please phone for admission prices and opening times: 01984 640377.

In Washford, ¼ mile S of A39
OS Map 181; ref ST 047407

DARTMOUTH CASTLE
DEVON

Jutting out into the narrow entrance of the Dart estuary, Dartmouth Castle was well placed to guard one of England's busiest ports. Although partly medieval, it was largely rebuilt in the late 14th century, and was one of the earliest castles to be constructed with artillery attack in mind. Fortifications were added over the centuries right up to the Second World War.

Open year-round. Please phone for admission prices and opening times: 01803 833588.

1 mile SE of Dartmouth off B3205
OS Map 202; ref SX 887503

FARLEIGH HUNGERFORD CASTLE
SOMERSET

Sir Thomas Hungerford acquired and fortified Farleigh manor in 1370, and over time it became Farleigh Hungerford Castle. Of the original castle, the two south towers, parts of the curtain wall, the outer gatehouse, and the 14th-century chapel and crypt remain. The chapel boasts some fine stained glass and wall paintings.

Open year-round. Please phone for admission prices and opening times: 01225 754026.

In Farleigh Hungerford, 3¹/₂ miles W of Trowbridge on A366
OS Map 173; ref ST 801576

LULWORTH CASTLE
DEVON

Lulworth Castle was built in 1608 as a hunting lodge, intended to attract James I to hunt in the Isle of Purbeck. It became a family seat later in the 17th century, set in beautiful parkland. Although it was gutted by fire in 1929, in the 1990s the exterior was restored, and the interior displays trace its history.

Open year-round. Owned and managed by the Lulworth Estate. Please phone for admission prices and opening times: 01929 400352.

In east Lulworth off B3070, 3 miles NE of Lulworth Cove
OS Map 194; ref SY 853822

MUCHELNEY ABBEY
SOMERSET

A monastery was reputedly established here by Ine, a 7th-century king of Wessex. It did not survive the Viking invasions, but the community was refounded in about 950. The abbey buildings were largely rebuilt in the 12th century and the foundations of these survive today, together with the fine 16th-century abbot's lodging.

Open 1 Apr–31 Oct. Please phone for admission prices and opening times: 01458 250664.

In Muchelney, 2 miles S of Langport via Huish Episcopi
OS Map 193; ref ST 429249

OKEHAMPTON CASTLE
DEVON

The extensive ruins of what was once the largest castle in Devon stand on a wooded spur high above the River Okement. Built soon after the Norman Conquest, it provided a dramatic symbol of the power of the newly arrived nobility. Major alterations were made in the early 14th century to transform it into an up-to-date lordly residence.

Open 1 Apr–30 Sep. Please phone for admission prices and opening times: 01984 640377.

1 mile SW of Okehampton town centre
OS Map 191; ref SX 583942

PORTLAND CASTLE
DORSET

Portland Castle is one of the best preserved of Henry VIII's great chain of coastal forts, built in the 1540s. It is planned like a segment of a circle, with the keep to the rear and a two-storey battery facing out to sea. It saw serious fighting during the Civil War, served as a seaplane station during the First World War, and was at the forefront of D-Day preparations in 1944.

Open 1 Apr–31 Oct. Please phone for admission prices and opening times: 01305 820539.

Overlooking Portland harbour in Castleton, Isle of Portland
OS Map 194; ref SY 685744

ROYAL CITADEL, PLYMOUTH
DEVON

This dramatic 17th-century fortress was built to counter a threatened Dutch invasion. Commissioned by Charles II, it is still in military use today, standing prominently on Plymouth Sound with the huge Devonport dockyard in its shadow. The magnificent Baroque gateway, built entirely of Portland stone, survives on Hoe Road.

Open May–Sep, by guided tour only. For details please email plymouthukbbg@hotmail.com

At E end of Plymouth Hoe
OS Map 201; ref SX 480538

SHERBORNE OLD CASTLE
DORSET

Queen Elizabeth I gave this 12th-century castle to Sir Walter Raleigh, but he seems to have preferred his purpose-built hunting lodge, the 'New Castle', which stands nearby. When General Fairfax laid siege to Sherborne in 1645 it was 16 days before the defending Royalists surrendered. The ruined south-west gatehouse and parts of the keep and encircling walls survive.

Open 1 Apr–31 Oct. Please phone for admission prices and opening times: 01935 812730.

¹/₂ mile E of Sherborne off B3145
OS Map 183; ref ST 648168

TOTNES CASTLE
DEVON

The town of Totnes is still dominated by the motte-and-bailey castle built by the Normans to keep the townspeople in order. The castle never saw battle, and the distinctive circular keep remains remarkably intact, one of the best preserved of its date. There are splendid views from the castle over the River Dart.

Open 1 Apr–31 Oct. Please phone for admission prices and opening times: 01803 864406.

In Totnes, on a hill overlooking the town
OS Map 202; ref SX 800605

INDEX

GENERAL BOOKS

M. Robertson, *Exploring England's Heritage: Dorset to Gloucestershire*, HMSO, 1992

A. Saunders, *Exploring England's Heritage: Devon and Cornwall*, HMSO, 1991

M. Todd, *A Regional History of England: The South West to AD 1000*, Longman, 1987

PREHISTORIC SITES

R. Bewley, *Prehistoric Settlements*, Batsford/English Heritage, 1994

M. Corbishley, T. Darvill and P. Stone, *Prehistory*, English Heritage, 2000

B. Cunliffe, *Iron Age Communities in Britain*, Routledge and Kegan Paul, 1978

T. C. Darvill, *Prehistoric Britain*, Batsford, 1987

M. Parker Pearson, *Bronze Age Britain*, Batsford/English Heritage, 1993

DEVON

Bayard's Cove Fort

R. Freeman, *Dartmouth and its Neighbours*, Phillimore, 1990

B. H. St J. O'Neill, 'Dartmouth Castle and other defences of Dartmouth Haven', *Archaeologia*, 85, 1935, pp. 129–57

Blackbury Camp

A. Young and K. Richardson, 'Report on the excavation of Blackberry Castle', *Proceedings of the Devon Archaeological Society*, 5, 1954–5, pp. 43–67

Dartmoor and its monuments (Grimspound, Houndtor, Lydford, Merrivale, Upper Plym Valley)

J. Butler, *Dartmoor Atlas of Antiquities*, 4 vols., Devon Books, 1991–4

Dartmoor National Park Authority, *A Guide to the Archaeology of Dartmoor*, Devon Books, 1996

S. Gerrard, *Dartmoor*, Batsford/English Heritage, 1997

T. Greeves, *The Archaeology of Dartmoor from the Air*, Dartmoor National Park/Devon Books, 1985

F. Griffith, *Devon's Past: An Aerial View*, Devon Books, 1988

R. Sale, *Dartmoor: The Official National Park Guide*, Pevensey Press/David and Charles, 2000

Kirkham House

P. Beacham (ed.), *Devon Building*, Devon Books, 1990

B. Cherry and N. Pevsner, *The Buildings of England: Devon*, Penguin, 1952–89

Kirkham House, English Heritage, 1985

Lydford

A. D. Saunders, *Lydford Saxon Town and Castle*, HMSO, 1964

A. D. Saunders, in *Medieval Archaeology*, 24, 1980, pp. 123–64

DORSET

Abbotsbury Abbey and St Catherine's Chapel

G. Coppack, *Abbeys and Priories*, English Heritage, 1990

L. Keen and C. Taylor, *St Catherine's Chapel at Abbotsbury and the Legend of the Saint*, 1999

Christchurch Castle and Norman House

Victoria History of Hampshire and the Isle of Wight, vol. 5, 1912, pp. 88–90

M. Wood, *Christchurch Castle*, Department of the Environment/HMSO, 1972

M. Wood, *The English Medieval House*, Bracken Books, 1985

Fiddleford Manor

H. C. Dashwood, 'Fiddleford', *Proceedings of the Dorset Natural History and Archaeological Society*, 16, 1895, pp. 55–8

J. Newman and N. Pevsner, *The Buildings of England: Dorset*, Penguin, 1972

Jordan Hill Roman Temple

A. Woodward, *Shrines and Sacrifice*, Batsford/English Heritage, 1992

Knowlton Church and Earthworks

A. Burl, *Prehistoric Henges*, Shire Publications, 1991

S. Burrow and J. Gale, 'Survey and excavation at Knowlton Rings, Woodland Parish, Dorset, 1993–5', *Proceedings of the Dorset Natural History and Archaeological Society*, 117, 1995, pp. 131–2

www.britarch.ac.uk

Maiden Castle

N. Sharples, *Maiden Castle: Excavations and Field Survey*, Batsford/English Heritage, 1991

Sir M. Wheeler, *Maiden Castle*, HMSO, 1972

Prehistoric monuments of Dorset (Kingston Russell, Knowlton, Maiden Castle, Winterbourne Nine Stones and Poor Lot Barrows)

J. Gale, *Prehistoric Dorset*, Tempus Publishing, 2003

SOMERSET

Dunster

Dunster Castle, Somerset, National Trust, 1990

E. Jervoise, *The Ancient Bridges of the South of England*, Architectural Press, 1930

N. Pevsner, *The Buildings of England: South and West Somerset*, Penguin, 1958

C. Pooley, *Old Crosses of Somerset*, Longman Green & Company, 1877

Glastonbury Tribunal

P. Rahtz, *Glastonbury*, Batsford/English Heritage, 1993

C. A. Ralegh Radford, *Glastonbury Tribunal*, DoE/English Heritage, 1977

Meare Fish House

M. Aston (ed.), *Medieval Fish, Fisheries and Fishponds in England*, BAR British Series, 182 (I and II), 1988

R. W. Dunning (ed.), *The Victoria History of Somerset*, vol 9, *Glastonbury and Somerset* (forthcoming)

Nunney Castle

Colin Platt, *The Castle in Medieval England and Wales*, Secker and Warburg, 1982

S. E. Rigold, *Nunney Castle*, London, 1956

Sir Bevil Grenville's Monument

J. Kingross, *Walking and Exploring the Battlefields of Britain*, David and Charles, 1988

M. Tolhurst, *The English Civil War*, English Heritage, 1992

Stanton Drew Stone Circles and Cove

A. Burl, *Prehistoric Henges*, Shire Publications, 1991

A. J. Clark, *Seeing Beneath the Soil*, Batsford, 1996

www.eng-h.gov.uk/archaeometry/StantonDrew

Stoney Littleton Long Barrow

L. V. Grinsell, *Barrows*, Shire Publications, 1984

L. V. Grinsell, *Stoney Littleton Long Barrow*, Department of the Environment/HMSO, 1978

FEATURES

A Bronze Age Landscape: Prehistoric Dartmoor

See under 'Dartmoor and its monuments', p. 94

Great Estates: Major Landowners of the South West

M. Aston, *Monasteries in the Landscape*, Tempus Publishing, 2000

J. H. Bettey, *Estates and the English Countryside*, Batsford, 1993

Medieval Monasteries in the South West

J. H. Bettey, *The Suppression of the Monasteries in the West Country*, Sutton Publishing, 1989

L. and J. Laing, *Medieval Britain*, Herbert Press, 1996

N. Saul (ed.), *The Oxford Illustrated History of Medieval England*, Oxford University Press, 1997

Writers and Artists of Devon, Dorset and Somerset

H. Brigstocke (ed.), *The Oxford Companion to Western Art*, Oxford University Press, 2001

C. Hardyment, *Literary Trails: Writers in their Landscapes*, National Trust, 2000

I. Ousby, *Blue Guide to Literary Britain and Ireland*, Black, 1985

Waterlogged Heritage: The Somerset Levels

B. and J. Coles, *Sweet Track to Glastonbury*, Thames and Hudson, 1986

J. M. Coles and B. J. Orme, *Prehistory of the Somerset Levels*, Somerset Levels Project, 1980

Useful websites relating to Devon, Dorset and Somerset

www.english-heritage.org.uk
(English Heritage)

www.britarch.ac.uk
(Council for British Archaeology)

www.dartmoor-npa.gov.uk
(Dartmoor National Park Authority)

www.dartmoor.co.uk
(Dartmoor Online)

dorsetcc.gov.uk
(Dorset County Council)

www.discoverdevon.com
(Discover Devon)

www.exmoor-nationalpark.gov.uk
(Exmoor National Park Authority)

www.nationaltrust.org.uk
(National Trust)

www.somerset.gov.uk/celebratingsomerset
(Somerset County Council)

www.visitsouthwest.co.uk or
www.westcountrynow.com
(South West Tourism)